The Train Stops Here

Frontispiece: Classification tracks, REA building, depot, and Gran Quivira Hotel, Clovis. Photo by Don Erb, courtesy of the Kansas State Historical Society, Topeka, Kansas.

THE TRAIN STOPS HERE

New Mexico's Railway Legacy

MARCI L. RISKIN

UNIVERSITY OF NEW MEXICO PRESS
ALBUQUERQUE

iv

Dedication

To David Moore,

who provided support,

patience, and punctuation,

as well as a little office in

Arbour Hill, Dublin, in which

I wrote this book.

LIBRARY OF CONGRESS CATALOGING-IN-PUBLICATION DATA

Riskin, Marci L., 1966–
The train stops here : New Mexico's railway legacy /
Marci L. Riskin.— 1st ed.
p. cm.
Includes bibliographical references and index.
ISBN 0-8263-3306-0 (cloth : alk. paper) —
ISBN 0-8263-3307-9 (pbk. : alk. paper)
1. Railroad stations—New Mexico—History.
2. Railroad stations—New Mexico—Pictorial works.
I. Title.
TF302.N49R57 2005
385.3'14—dc22
2004028040

DESIGN AND COMPOSITION: *Mina Yamashita*

Contents

Acknowledgments

This book is the culmination of almost ten years of research, and I would like to express my thanks to the many people who made it a reality.

Several people accompanied me around the state visiting New Mexico's remaining railroad structures. Sharon Wharton, Glen Gollrad, and Jud Cervenak donated not only their time but also their photographs to my dream. Glen also provided valuable research into the details of railway operations.

Gaylon Bobo of Portales, Virginia Jones of Capitan, Clovis historian Don McAlavy, J. N. "Shnooks" McDaniel, Fort Sumner historian Bob Parsons, Bob Sarr of the Santa Fe Southern, Clovis Depot Model Train Museum owner Phil Williams, and others shared their memories of New Mexico's railroad past.

David Moore not only furnished an office in Dublin and allowed me the time to write this book, he also greatly improved the quality of the manuscript with his admirable editing skills.

And finally, Fred Friedman, former chief of the New Mexico State Highway and Transportation Department's Rail Bureau, commissioned a study of New Mexico's railroad depots, which was my first introduction to the rich railroad heritage in the state. He is the reason this book exists at all.

Fig. 1. The Alvarado Hotel is demolished, February 1970. Photo by Gordon Ferguson, courtesy of the Museum of New Mexico, neg. no. 58706.

PART ONE

Railroading's Heyday

Historic Weight and Romantic Spirit

Why Railroad Buildings Matter

On February 13, 1970, the Santa Fe Railway demolished Albuquerque's Alvarado Hotel. The railroad wanted $1.5 million for the vacant property, but the small group of local residents fighting to save the structure was unable to raise the money. In the months and years that followed, New Mexicans mourned the loss of the 1902 landmark, which had provided not only an identity for the city but also a place for the community to gather. A Harvey hotel designed by Santa Fe Railway architect Charles Whittlesey in the Mission Revival style, the building was architecturally and historically significant. But its place in the wider history of railroad development in the United States added another layer to the loss.

From the first American railroad journeys in the early nineteenth century, railroads quickly became an integral part of life in the United States, particularly in the undeveloped western region. Settlements there were troubled by unique problems: isolation and inadequate provisions, hostile American Indian communities, and a lack of water—barring the occasional flood. These were obstacles for the railroads as well. With the large amount of initial capital required to build a railroad, a new line was a daunting financial risk, and many failed. But those that succeeded not only made money, they also helped define the West, populating it and linking it to the rest of the United States.

In the immense and isolated territory of New Mexico, the railroads' effect was striking. Trade routes such as the Camino Real to Mexico, established in the sixteenth century, and the 1821 Santa Fe Trail to Kansas had made the territory important for commerce, and it was included in many early railroad surveys. But it was also sparsely populated until construction camps, sidings, and new towns emerged along the tracks to service the railroad. Many of New Mexico's cities, including Carlsbad, Raton, Clovis, and Gallup were initially established as railroad stops. Other towns, like Grenville, Elida, and Whitewater, were once listed prominently on railroad timetables, but are now practically ghost towns. La Mesilla and Las Cruces competed zealously for the railroads' attention; that Las Cruces absorbed its once-larger neighbor to become one of the largest cities in the state is evidence of the railroads' power.

In addition to influencing the pattern of settlement, the railroads also determined the routes of roads and highways. Towns were often founded primarily to service the railroad with water stops and repair crews; later they would service the highway with motels and gas stations. In the West, the road is an experience in itself; the idea of the road trip began as a railroad trip: after miles of rangeland, where the only sign of human activity is a fence of piñon branches and barbed wire and a few cattle, arrival at the depot was, and still is, an occasion.

For railroads' extensive impact on the expansion of the West and the appearance and location of towns, it is worth preserving our railroad heritage. Realizing this, in 2002, the City of Albuquerque reconstructed the Alvarado in its historic location at the corner of First Street and Central (once Railroad) Avenue. The noble intent of those who led the project was to adhere to the concept of transportation; the new Alvarado was to be a transportation hub for Albuquerque—in essence, a $7 million bus depot.

But as well as their great historical significance, railroads had a profound effect on the lives of individuals. In its prime, the railroad station served as an informal town center. The whistle of an approaching train, the smell of creosote, and the shade of a covered platform on a hot day came to represent not only the journey but a sense of community within a town. Historian Bob Parsons captured the notion with clarity: "Used to be you'd go up the depot just to see who came in and who was going out and what the news was."[1] And so, while the Alvarado Transportation Center borrows some of the look of the original, the new structure does not revive its spirit. The Alvarado Hotel was beloved not only for its quatrefoil details and Spanish arcades but also as a place where generations of Albuquerque residents gathered for graduation parties and proms, attended wedding receptions, and celebrated with romantic dinners.

In addition to the historical imperative, there is a more sentimental reason for preservation. In an era when the idea of communal travel has been nearly lost, railroads are still in our collective soul. When people learn that you're writing a book on railroads, they tell their tales, their personal connection to this shared history. Our grandfathers were engineers or worked in section gangs or laid rails. Our parents took the train to boot camp or to college or to start a better life. This romantic notion of date nails, coal-fired steam engines, icehouses, narrow gauge, and Fred Harvey lunchrooms adds another dimension of value to the historic structures of the railroad. The broad history of the buildings is made more meaningful by the personal stories.

The intent of this book is to explore both the history and the romance of New Mexico's remaining railroad depots and other structures—everything but the trains. To provide context, the book includes a brief history of railroad development, a description of the architectural features of New Mexico's railroad buildings, and an overview of how the rolling stock, track, structures, and workers combined to transport both people and goods. This background should help answer the questions that may arise when on a visit to a railyard: what is that strangely shaped train car carrying, how is that twisted piece of metal used, or why are the bricks on the platform stamped with the single word *Coffeyville*?

Railroads are about transportation and movement, but they depend on numerous structures that go nowhere. As time and the train rush by, the depots, the coal tipples, the turntables, and water towers stay still, a testament to our past. The intent of this book is to pay homage to these places and to highlight what remains of the railroad legacy in New Mexico.

CHAPTER TWO

Track, Steam, Stations, and Laws

The Evolution of the Modern Railroad

Evolution of the Locomotive

Several components of the modern railroad were in place even before steam power was introduced. The Romans constructed grooved roadbeds of paved stones that allowed carts and chariots to carry heavy loads even in inclement weather. Later, sixteenth- and seventeenth-century coal mines in northeast England used wooden planks with animal-powered wagons to carry the extracted coal. In the eighteenth century the wooden track was replaced by thin metal strips that were more durable and could carry more weight. Later in the century in South Wales, short segments of cast-iron track were mounted to stone blocks, replacing the metal strips. First cast in 1767 by Colebrookdale Iron Works, these track segments, called "plateways," had a flange to keep the wheels in line, another significant improvement. Tougher wrought-iron rails were then used; they were less brittle, but softer, and still not ideal. Around the same time, the collieries first began to link several wagons together to haul more coal at once, and the concept of the train was born. Throughout the eighteenth century, however, these track systems were used only by horse-drawn carts.

However, people were also learning to manipulate and harness the power of steam. The first modern steam engine was built by engineer Thomas Newcomen in 1705. Others made improvements to Newcomen's invention, including James Watt's 1763 addition of a crank and flywheel to provide rotary motion. Steam engines were later connected to a winch to pull wagons of coal or other mineral ores; these were straight pulls, however, and did not allow for a curved track. Throughout the eighteenth century, steam engines were used mainly to pump water out of mines, and whether pulling or pumping, the engine itself was stationary. Despite the limited uses of steam power, visionary inventors saw the possibilities of using it for transportation. Richard Trevithick invented the first practical self-propelled steam locomotive around 1803; the steam engine turned a crank to pull a rope, as in the winch scenario, but it was placed on a wheeled cart to move itself. In 1812, the first commercial steam locomotive was used by the English collieries to haul coal and heavy equipment.

Also in the early 1800s, passenger transportation began to take advantage of track previously used only by commercial freight; however, the trackbound cars were drawn by horses. The Stockton & Darlington Railway, the first public steam line, was naturally aimed at freight rather than passengers; its primary goal was to introduce a less expensive means of transporting coal within the region. Chief engineer George Stephenson, who would become a legend in railroad design, designed both the locomotive and the track. He introduced a major improvement: attaching the flange to the wheel instead of the rail, which solved the problem of debris collecting along the flanged track. It also was much easier for carts and carriages (and later, cars) to cross, and is the configuration still used today. The first journey, in September 1825, hauled sixty-eight tons of coal twenty-one miles, from Shildon to Stockton. The line was put into use immediately, but although it accommodated passenger cars, they were still powered by live horses rather than iron ones.

Liverpool & Manchester

Only five years later, though, passengers and freight shared the same public railroad line. The world's first real railroad, carrying both freight and passengers on a regular schedule, was proposed to link Manchester, the center of England's textile industry, with Liverpool, its most important northern port, to reduce the cost of transporting raw materials and finished goods. The Liverpool & Manchester Railway devised a unique way of finding an engine: it held a locomotive design competition. Each entry had to pull a load of three times its own weight at a speed of at least ten miles per hour. The Liverpool & Manchester was a favorite story of the press in the months leading up to the contest. The *Quarterly Review* supported the railroad, but warned about the proposed speed: "What can be more palpably absurd than the prospect held out of locomotives travelling twice as fast as stagecoaches! We trust that Parliament will, in all railways it may sanction, limit the speed to eight or nine miles an hour."[1] The competition was won with an even faster speed of fourteen miles per hour by an engine appropriately called The Rocket, built by George Stephenson's son Robert. On September 15, 1830, in front of a crowd of dignitaries, it made its first thirty-one-mile journey.

The Liverpool & Manchester Railway was a great success. The cost of transportation was reduced, and passenger service soon followed freight. But as the railway's secretary and treasurer, Henry Booth, noted in 1830, "Perhaps the most striking result produced by the completion of this railway, is the sudden change which has been effected in our ideas of time

and space. What was quick is now slow; what was distant is now near."[2] The Industrial Revolution, which resulted in a myriad of technological advances, was responsible for the development of railroads, but railroads, in turn, facilitated further industrialization.

Early U.S. Railways

In the United States, progress was slower. The first use of a steam locomotive on a track was not until 1825, when John Stevens, formerly an officer during the Revolutionary War, ran a locomotive on a circular track that he had built in Hoboken, New Jersey. This was purely an experiment; it was not until three years later that the Delaware & Hudson Canal Company began to explore the idea of steam-powered locomotives for use on their commercial railroad in Honesdale, Pennsylvania. They sent a young engineer, Horatio Allen, to England to buy three locomotives from Foster, Rastrick & Co., based in Stourbridge, a manufacturing town on the River Stour west of Birmingham. The engines arrived in New York in May of 1829, and the goal was to run one on July 4, but the railroad was not completed until August. On August 8, the Stourbridge Lion, decorated with the distinctive lions' heads for which it was named, became the first full-size steam locomotive to run on a commercial line in the United States, four years after the Stockton & Darlington line was put into service in England. Allen served as engineer, and the locomotive reached a speed of ten miles an hour, considered a triumph, but the six-ton engine was too heavy for the Delaware & Hudson's track; the track strained under its weight, and the Stourbridge Lion was never run on it again. The Lion's two twins were never used as anything but stationary power engines.

In 1830, the Baltimore & Ohio built the "Old

Fig. 2. Ellicott City Station, 1999. Photo by William Eric McFadden.

Main Line" from Baltimore to Ellicott's Mills (now Ellicott City), a town producing iron and milling flour on the Patapsco River. The line opened on May 24 using horse-drawn cars, but there was always an interest in using steam engines instead, though skeptics doubted that steam engines could be faster than stagecoaches. On August 30, the owner of a stagecoach line challenged Peter Cooper's engine, the Tom Thumb, which earned its name from its diminutive size, to a race on the Old Main Line. The steam engine was in the lead, but a slipped belt brought the Tom Thumb to a stop, and the stagecoach horses crossed the finish line first. The Baltimore & Ohio soon used locomotives for hauling freight and then for passenger service. Though the United States lagged consistently behind England in railroad development, it soon exceeded England in miles of track.

The First Railroad Stations

Since a new building type was needed for this new industry, the first railroad stations closely followed the development of the railroads. Their primary function was to provide sheltered places to wait and buy tickets. The first English station was built in 1830 at Crown Street in Liverpool, and the first American station was built a year later in Ellicott's Mills, Maryland, at the crossroads of the Patapsco River and the Old National Highway. It is still standing. These buildings had many of the features of railroad stations to come, including waiting and ticketing areas and a platform. Both were one-sided depots with arrival and departure via a platform on one side of the tracks. Although later designs employed a more complex track configuration, this cost-effective arrangement was the only one ever used in New Mexico.

Ellicott's Mills was an unpretentious stone building, and indeed most early American stations were basic and utilitarian, since railroads spent their initial money on track systems and trains. An existing pub or an inn could easily provide the required passenger services. But railroad companies eventually realized the importance of marketing an attractive image, and grand railroad stations were constructed to serve important American East Coast cities. New York's Grand Central Station, built in 1869, was as magnificent and well detailed as its European counterparts. As arrival and departure from terminals became an event, railroad stations became the center of community in most cities, and later buildings reflect that level of importance. Even in New Mexico, where railroad stations were small and simple, they were still often the most imposing buildings in town.

Building the U.S. Railroad System

Like the highway system that would follow, the development of the railroad system in the United States was highly supported and subsidized by the government. In 1850 the U.S. public domain was 1.4 billion acres, but this land was considered unusable and difficult to sell due to a lack of transportation. The prevailing thought was that westward expansion was critical for military security and national unity and that, since the land had little or no value without a method of transportation, part could be given away to increase the value of the rest. Senator William R. King, in the Senate debate on the passage of the railroad land grant bill, argued against the objection that too many acres were being granted: "[I]t is a great quantity; but it will be there for five hundred years; and unless some mode [of transportation] of the kind proposed be adopted, it will never command ten cents."[3] As it had done before with wagon roads and canals, the government gave away land to encourage and assist the building of railroads. The passage of the Pacific Railroad Act into law by President Lincoln in 1862,

including land grants and loans as incentives, ensured that a transcontinental railroad would be built.

Under the Pacific Railroad Act, the government made grants to the railroads of six square-mile sections of public domain or American Indian land for each mile of track. The land was distributed in a checkerboard pattern so that much federal land remained; the pattern can still be seen on ownership maps today. Within the Federal Railroad Land Grant program, railroads received a total of 131,350,534 acres.

The Department of the Interior also acted in the railroads' interest when it extinguished American Indian claims to land along the railroad routes. During the debates in the 1840s regarding the route of the transcontinental railroad, the rights of American Indians were ignored. When they were compensated, the government paid only $4 or $5 an acre, and even that was paid in U.S. Treasury credits rather than in currency.

With this considerable help, the railroads quickly became established. The first transcontinental railroad, originally estimated to take ten years to build, took only four. The rails joined at Promontory Point, Utah, on May 10, 1869. By 1890 there were 163,500 miles of track, and the railroad industry drove the economy, providing employment to thousands (the combined payroll of the 1,800,000 railway workers in 1916 was $1.5 billion) and consuming U.S. products such as coal and steel. More than this, the railroads helped to unify a vast and disjointed country. What was once a four- to six-month journey now took merely six days. But the railroad also brought other unifying benefits.

Railroad By-Products

The first railroad by-product was a national, transcontinental telegraph system, developed in tandem with the track. This had a profound effect on communication; the vast United States could be governed from one location.

Another by-product was the adoption of standard time zones. Before the railroads, the country was not just divided by large distances between settlements, it also had 1,183 separate time zones in around eighty separate time regions. For safety and efficiency in coordinating the movement of trains, the railroads created standard railway time zones in 1883. These included Atlantic Railway Time Zone, Eastern Railway Time Zone, Central Railway Time Zone, Mountain Railway Time Zone, and Pacific Railway Time Zone. A writer for the *Indianapolis Sentinel* lamented in November of that year: "Railroad time, it appears, is to be the time of the future. And so, people will now have to marry and die by railroad time. Ministers will preach by railroad time, and banks will be required to open and close by the same time. The sun is no longer the boss of the job."[4] He was proven right, when the U.S. government adopted these zones in 1918, eliminating the term "Railway" and instituting Atlantic, Eastern, Central, Mountain, and Pacific time.

A final by-product unintended by the railroad was the new legislation enacted by the U.S. government to control the shady behavior by the railroad industry, which they had all but encouraged a few years earlier. The profit-driven railroad companies could be as corrupt as some contemporary corporations. There were few regulations regarding the conduct of corporations, partly because before the late nineteenth century, there were few industries large and competitive enough to warrant legislation. But eventually, the cutthroat practices of the railroad companies led to an anti-railroad movement based on public indignation at malpractice and abuse.

Grassroots political organizations such as the Granger Movement, founded originally for social and educational purposes, became more active after the Panic of 1873, an economic depression caused by unchecked growth and speculation, including the overbuilding of the nation's railroad network, which led to the failure of major companies. Jay Cooke & Co., the banking firm that financed the Northern Pacific, was the first to declare bankruptcy and close its doors. Granger laws were passed in the Midwest setting maximum railroad rates and establishing state railroad commissions to administer the new legislation. Though these laws were challenged, in 1876 the U.S. Supreme Court upheld the constitutionality of governmental regulation of private utilities devoted to public use.

The Interstate Commerce Commission (ICC), established in 1887, further limited the power of the railroad industry, regulating companies engaged in transportation between states. The ICC's jurisdiction was gradually extended to all carriers except airplanes by 1940. Most of its functions now reside with the Department of Transportation and the National Transportation Safety Board.

The anti-railroad movement continued, however, gaining force in the 1890s. In 1892, the Populist Party entered the presidential election with a platform featuring freedom from "railroad oppression." In 1901, Frank Norris's anti-railroad book *The Octopus* was published.[5] The railroad's response to the bad press was public relations and new buildings. These buildings remain as evidence; they have something to say about both the good and the bad of our railroad past.

Fig. 3. Santa Fe Trail wagon ruts near Fort Union, ca. 1900. Courtesy of the Museum of New Mexico, neg. no. 12845.

CHAPTER THREE

The Railroad Transforms the Territory

Before the Railroads

While the Industrial Revolution had transformed eastern U.S. cities into vibrant centers of commerce, New Mexico was still remote and largely undeveloped. Mexico had only recently won self rule from Spain (with the Treaty of Córdoba, signed on September 21, 1821) when Colonel Stephen Kearney arrived in Las Vegas during the Mexican-American War, with orders from the U.S. government to conquer New Mexico and California. On August 15, 1846, from Las Vegas's historic plaza, he proclaimed victory in New Mexico. "I have come amongst you by the orders of my government, to take possession of your country, and extend over it the laws of the United States," he declared. "We come amongst you as friends—not as enemies; as protectors—not as conquerors."[1] The pronouncement was slightly premature but was made official in 1848 when the Treaty of Guadalupe Hidalgo ended the war with Mexico by transferring Mexican lands to the United States, including what would one day be Utah, Colorado, Arizona, California, and New Mexico. New Mexico was officially declared a territory in 1850, less than twenty years before the first transcontinental railroad. In 1860 the area was divided to create a new Territory of Arizona, because it was impractical for Arizonans to travel to the territorial capital, Santa Fe, to conduct official business.

Although New Mexico was sparsely populated and there were many American Indian raids, the region was an important location for trade routes and cattle trails. The sixteenth-century Camino Real de Tierra Adentro linked Santa Fe with Mexico City; the corridor is still active today in its incarnation as Interstate 25. Trading increased in 1821 with the first journey on the Santa Fe Trail from Independence, Missouri. The trail went through Council Grove, Kansas, into Bent's Fort, Colorado, and through the Raton Pass to Santa Fe. Stagecoach routes such as the Butterfield Overland mail route were developed to bring travelers and mail to the new U.S. territories. After the end of the Civil War cattle drives began, including the Magdalena Stock Driveway and the Goodnight-Loving Trail.

New Mexico's First Railroads

Vast parts of the region remained unconnected to this network. Overall, New Mexico changed little in the fifty years after the establishment of the Santa Fe Trail. But the railroad companies had not overlooked Santa Fe's status as a trade center. New Mexico figured prominently in the Pacific railroad surveys of 1853 to 1856, but it was not until 1878 that the tracks reached the state. That year, two companies, both with the goal of building transcontinental railroads, fought for the best route through the mountainous region along the Colorado–New Mexico border. With its moderate grades and shallow curves, Raton Pass was promising, but it lay in difficult terrain. The pass was the original route of the Santa Fe Trail, but it was unimproved and dangerous and fell out favor, replaced by the Cimarron Cutoff, which entered New Mexico from the panhandle of Oklahoma. The pass, now called the Mountain Route, became viable once again when "Uncle Dick" Wootton cleared the land, graded the road, and constructed a toll bridge.

In 1878, both the Atchison, Topeka & Santa Fe and the Denver & Rio Grande railroads surveyed Raton Pass, but neither filed their locations with the Department of the Interior, leaving it open to whichever company claimed if first. As the first to initiate construction, the Santa Fe established its right, and though the Denver & Rio Grande built elsewhere in the territory, the Santa Fe would always be the primary player in New Mexico railroading.

After the Raton Pass route was built, the Santa Fe and other railroads extended their track quickly despite complex landforms that made New Mexico difficult for surveying. The Guadalupe and Sacramento Mountains in the south, the Sangre de Cristo Mountains in the north, and the San Juan Mountains in the far north were obstacles that were usually avoided. Instead, the railroads often followed already-established trade routes, for example, the Atlantic & Pacific following the Zuni/Rio Grande Trail and the El Paso & Southwestern using the Butterfield Overland mail route in the southwest. Gentle grades could also be found along rivers; the Santa Fe chose to follow the Camino Real, which trails the Rio Grande. The southern part of the Pecos Valley Railroad followed the course of the Pecos River, a route used by the Goodnight-Loving cattle trail.

In such a sparsely populated state, the immediate goal of most railroads was not passenger or freight but exploiting the region's rich mineral resources such as gold, silver, and copper and satisfying the railroad's constant need for coal for fuel. The commerce and daily life in New Mexico was transformed. The coal industry—subterranean coal in the San Juan basin in the northwest, bituminous soft coal near Raton and Capitan, and hard coal near Cerrillos—was the first to expand. But sheep and cattle ranches developed as well, and farmers in the Rio Grande valley shipped their produce east. Later, uranium and oil fields were discovered in the northwest and southeast, and potash—used for commercial fertilizers—was mined in the southeast. As New Mexico's resources were utilized, access to consumer goods also increased. The railroad brought previously unseen products from the East, like tin roofs and brick, and brand-name items such as soaps and sewing machines.

Anglo Settlement

New Mexico was finally connected to the rest of the country with transcontinental lines that led west to California and east to Chicago and beyond. With transportation in place, the U.S. government enacted legislation to bring settlers to the West. President Abraham Lincoln signed the first Homestead Act in 1862, and it took effect on January 1, 1863. The act ended seventy years of controversy over the fate of public lands. The Free-Soil Party, and eventually Lincoln's Republican Party, wanted to distribute the land for free as a means of preventing slavery in the territories. The southern states opposed this, but when they seceded from the United States in 1861, the deadlock was eliminated and the act was adopted. Under the Homestead Act, claimants settled 270 million acres, 10 percent of the area of the United States. Each claim was 160 acres, and settlers were required to make specific improvements (build a home, dig a well, plow ten acres, and fence a specified amount of land) and live there for five years. The only money required was a filing fee. The Homestead Act, which rapidly populated the American West, remained in effect until 1976, even though most

Fig. 4. White Oaks school-house, ca. 2000. Photo by author.

of the viable land was gone by 1908.

Later acts, such as the Desert Land Act of 1877, were aimed at settling the less desirable arid regions of the West, including New Mexico. The Homestead Act of 1909 raised the size of the claim from 160 to 320 acres, but in recognition that much of western land did not have enough water for proper farming, the 1916 Stock Raising Homestead Act raised the grant to 640 acres, a viable size for grazing.

It was the spread of the railroad network, however, more than these incentives, that settled New Mexico. In many ways, the history of the railroad in New Mexico is the history of the development of the territory itself during the late nineteenth and early twentieth centuries. The railroad affected the location and appearance of New Mexico's towns, the direction of New Mexico's highways, the style of its architecture, and its strong identity with its American Indian population. It brought people and goods, and, ultimately, a different culture—an American culture that

was an amalgam of all the places the railroad traveled, a culture that did not even exist before the railroad brought the elements together.

The Fate of New Mexican Towns in the Railroad Era

In 1878, on the eve of the introduction of railroading in New Mexico, there were few towns in the territory, and most of those were located along significant trade routes such as the Santa Fe Trail or the region's primary source of water, the Rio Grande.

But pre-railroad prosperity did not ensure survival in the post-railroad era. Many thriving towns faded when they were bypassed by railroad lines. White Oaks, now a famous ghost town, was once home to a thousand residents, a notable population by western standards of that era. It boasted gold-mining operations, newspapers, and stagecoach stops, and it was home to New Mexico's first state governor. In the late 1890s at least five railroads (including the Santa

Fe Railway and the El Paso & Northeastern) were projected to extend to White Oaks from El Paso. However, the town was too confident of securing a stop and greedily held out for higher land prices for the railroad right-of-way. This strategy failed, as it almost always did; a new town could materialize only a few miles away to serve the railroad's needs. The El Paso & Northeastern revised their survey and extended a branch line from Carrizozo to Capitan, bypassing White Oaks by ten miles. The town withered as the mines ran out of ore.

The railroad altered the fate of well-established cities as well as more recently founded towns. Santa Fe, the territorial capital and an important trade center, was served only by a railroad spur, built in 1880 from the Santa Fe Railway. The city was large enough to survive what was then a crisis. As well as the question of why the Santa Fe had not run its main line through the town whose name they had borrowed, there was also much conjecture at the time about when the capital could be connected to the state's second major railroad, the Denver & Rio Grande, which reached only as far south as Española; the link was not made until 1887. Santa Fe has flourished, but it is no coincidence that Albuquerque, at the crossroads of New Mexico's major railroad systems and now highways, is by far the largest city in the state.

Even with the advantage of being served by main lines, some cities were divided in two by track built too far from an established downtown. Railroad routes were determined by cost and effort, so it was not uncommon to miss an obvious downtown stop to avoid a difficult river crossing or to follow more gentle grades. But the unintended consequence was a new neighborhood to serve the railroad's needs and provide for passengers. In Albuquerque, tracks were laid

a few miles east of the plaza, which had thrived for over a century as the center of the local economy. Today the distance seems minimal, but in 1880 the result was a new "town" of saloons, hotels, and other railroad-related enterprises. The plaza is now an area called Old Town, and the railroad's New Town is now simply known as downtown Albuquerque.

Despite a major effect on New Mexico's existing towns and cities, the railroads' most profound impact was on the new towns that developed along the tracks—many of New Mexico's present-day commercial centers have railroad origins. Most resulted from the need for water, fuel, and maintenance railroad stops at regular intervals. In the East, where towns were closer together, natural stops already existed. In New Mexico, where there were miles and miles of grassland and rolling hills, a section house was erected for the crew that maintained the rails, or a "temporary" construction camp was erected to facilitate trestle building. In these remote areas, this was enough to give birth to a town.

With offers of inexpensive land, people were enticed to settle in rural areas, and towns such as these grew quickly, becoming rowdy places with brothels, saloons, and gunfights. The expression "hell on wheels" was a reference to the brothels and gambling dens that were operated from railcars moving to chaotic new railroad towns where they hoped to find customers. A railroad stop informally called Six Shooter Siding was named for its copious gunfights—it would later become Tucumcari. Many of the towns that grew from railroad camps got their names from the local station agent or from prominent railroad company officials. Gallup was named for a railroad paymaster, and Grants was named for the contractors hired to lay the track. Often the railroad laid out new town sites on the land grants

Fig. 5. Railroad grade between Moriarty and Stanley, 2001. Photo by author.

given to them by the federal government, with the goal of generating additional income to subsidize rail-building. Within these towns, the railroads often called main arteries Main Street or Grand Avenue, with Main leading away from the depot. One example is Mountainair, with its handsome concrete and stucco depot anchoring Main Street.

The most convincing evidence of the railroads' effect on New Mexican settlement is the population boom: the region's inhabitants tripled from 1880 to 1920.

Transportation Networks

Just as cattle trails and trade and stage routes determined the locations of railroad lines, the railroads determined the path of the highways to follow. Some highways were even built directly on old railroad grades. Where the railroads still existed during construction of a new road, the highways run parallel. Where the railroad was abandoned, its raised bed, with gaps at missing trestles, can often be seen on the side of highways, grown over with native grasses—the familiar shape that reminds us that once railroads were everywhere.

A New Style

In addition to affecting the development of New Mexico's towns, the arrival of the railroad altered the appearance of the buildings within those towns. Before 1880, New Mexico's buildings were mostly utilitarian, built with locally available materials such as adobe bricks plastered with mud, which had to be reapplied often to prevent crumbling of the walls beneath. The flat roofs were at odds with sometimes heavy snowfall, but in keeping with the local building tradition. The railroad brought materials previously unseen from the East, such as tin and clay-fired brick, which were immediately used in construction. The brick provided a surface that did not have to be replastered year after year, and the tin was used to

Fig. 6. San Francisco Street, Santa Fe, ca. 1877. Photo by Benjamin H. Gurnsey, courtesy of the Museum of New Mexico, neg. no. 14624.

create pitched roofs that easily shed snow and rain.

Eastern architectural styles were imported as well, but applied with a regional flair. An adobe structure with a metal gable roof is still a common sight in New Mexico, and when new, larger windows with paned divisions were set into adobe walls with a brick cornice, the composite was called Territorial style.

The imported styles profoundly changed the character of towns such as Las Vegas, which still has its stately brick buildings from the railroad era. Before the railroad, Santa Fe's plaza was a collection of mostly one-story, flat-roofed adobe structures with *portales*, as shown in this photo of San Francisco Street taken in 1877, with the St. Francis Cathedral under construction. The city embraced the new materials offered by the railroad and only a few years later was completely rebuilt in a regional Eastern Brick style. The plaza's railroad-era buildings have since been remade with coats of plaster and added portales, but they retain their basic forms.

New Mexico Discovers Its Strongest Asset

The adoption of eastern styles and materials was reconsidered around the turn of the twentieth century, when the Santa Fe Railway saw the potential of the American Indian culture as a marketing tool. It had not been much earlier that the railroads had built their track through previously isolated American Indian communities. Now the railroad made regular tourist stops at locations such as Laguna Pueblo to allow railroad passengers to buy American Indian handcrafts, pots, and rugs.

The Santa Fe Railway was primarily a southwestern railroad. It and the Fred Harvey Company, which provided hotels and meals to Santa Fe passengers, began to promote the American Southwest as an exotic destination, tying their identities to the American Indian culture. Their advertising used American Indian symbols and images, and the architecture of the railroad depots in the West continued the theme with a unique style that drew on elements from American Indian and Spanish culture. The motif was carried through to the china in the dining cars; on the Super Chief running between Chicago and Los Angeles, the dinnerware in the mid-1930s incorporated patterns from Mimbreno Indian pottery. Even the names of the trains were borrowed from New Mexico's American Indian tribes and pueblos and included a dining car called the Cochiti, a lounge car called the Acoma, and sleeping cars called Oraibi, Taos, Laguna, Isleta, and Navajo.

The result of the intense marketing was an increase in railroad travel, particularly in tourist travel. The railroad, in turn, capitalized on this highly profitable tourist trade. At the turn of the century the Museum of Southwest Arts and Crafts was established, located in the Fred Harvey Indian Building at Albuquerque's Alvarado Hotel, adjacent to the depot. This was an important tourist stop, with live demonstrations and fine art for sale. But it is also an example of how the symbiotic promotion of railroad and tourism affected the places being toured. The Fred Harvey Indian Building organization commissioned crafts from American Indian artists based on what was popular, even suggesting new colors and styles for jewelry, textiles, and pottery. These creations are often mistakenly considered to be authentic examples of traditional American Indian design.

Not only the railroad but eventually New Mexico itself embraced its American Indian roots. As well as contributing to the region's strong tricultural—American Indian, Spanish, and Anglo—identity, American Indian culture has brought tourists to New Mexico.

PART TWO
The Railroad System

CHAPTER FOUR

Divisions, Sections, and the Five-Man Train Crew

Operational Considerations

E ven though railroad depots are historically important, attractive, and worthy of a visit in their own
right, the railroad is above all a system in which all of
the components—track, trains, and structures—work
together in concert. Attention to nearby buildings,
track, sights, smells, and sounds can only enhance the
experience of visiting a depot or railyard. With this in
mind, this chapter provides information about the railroad as a whole to answer some of the questions that
people may have during their explorations.

Operations

In a typical day, a train crew in the late nineteenth century traveled 100 to 150 miles along the line. For this
reason, railroads are divided into 100-mile operating
segments called divisions. Division points mark the
beginning and end of each division and contain major
railyards for the service and repair of locomotives. In
the days of the steam locomotive, the repair buildings
in the railyard included an engine house or roundhouse
to shelter locomotives during repair, coal towers for
providing fuel, and water tanks for watering the
engines. The division points were regular stops on the
line and therefore also served transportation needs

with passenger depots, freight depots, Railway Express Agency offices, and lunchrooms or hotels. As administrative centers, division points also had railroad company offices within the depot building or in a separate office building and sometimes a company reading room where the train crew could take breaks. At large division points such as Albuquerque, a railroad hospital was located a short distance from the yard.

New Mexico's division points included Gallup, Raton, Vaughn, Clovis, Chama, and, of course, Albuquerque. Now that communications have improved and trains are faster, division points are much farther apart. New methods of managing the railroad have made old buildings obsolete, but some of the numerous buildings that were once required to operate the railroad can still be seen.

Divisions are further subdivided into administrative districts, now called subdivisions. But in the past, when divisions were smaller, they were divided into sections. A section was the length of track, between ten and thirty miles, that could be maintained and repaired by a small gang of four to six workers, the most that fit on a handcar, a small wheeled car fitted to the rails that was propelled by hand to carry workers and materials along the rails. This workforce, called the section crew, spent their days riding up and down the rails in the handcar keeping their section of the track functional. The maintenance of main lines has since been mechanized, but on branch lines the track is still maintained the traditional way, just as it was 150 years ago, with a small track crew and simple tools.

Roles and Responsibilities

The main concern of railroad companies from their inception has always been safety. This is primarily because a train, with its incredible momentum, cannot be stopped in time to avoid something sighted on the track, including other trains. At first the United States adopted a timetable method to ensure that only one train occupied the track at a time. This later evolved into the timetable and train order method, T&TO, so that timetables could be overriden en route by train orders issued by station agents along the line. And, as the railroad evolved, centralized traffic control (CTC) was used. Now, railroads can be run with fewer employees, but there are still many tasks that must be performed to keep the system functioning. Basic positions in a railroad company are administrative, engineering, maintenance and repair, and the train crew.

The division head or superintendent leads the administrative arm of a railroad, supervising other administrators, including the trainmaster (in charge of traffic on the line), the terminal trainmaster (in charge of railyard traffic), the dispatcher (in charge of transmitting instructions for the movement of trains), the road foremen (in charge of locomotives), and the station agents (responsible for local stations). In the past, the railroad also employed a paymaster, who often moved up and down on the line in a special car distributing wages.

The engineering department is responsible for constructing and maintaining track and depots and other structures. Portions of track were maintained by a four- to six-person section crew that removed and replaced worn rail or ties and added additional ballast. Members of a section crew received $1 a day for their work in the 1870s.

The mechanical division is in charge of the maintenance and repair of locomotives, usually performed at division points. Among other jobs, there were machinists to fabricate replacement parts, blacksmiths to repair locomotive frames, and boilermakers to service boilers. These were dangerous jobs that often resulted in injury. Other railyard tasks were supervised by the terminal trainmaster. During the days of steam locomotives, engine watchmen kept water in the boiler and enough fire in the firebox to move locomotives in the yard. Hostlers moved engines into the roundhouse or engine house for repairs.

The work on the train was performed by the train crew. A traditional five-person crew included a conductor, engineer, fireman, brakeman, and rear brakeman. The conductor, in charge of the train, coordinated the activity of the train crew from the rear car of the train, from which the entire train could be surveyed. On the Santa Fe Railway in the 1870s, a conductor received a wage of $60 a month. The engineer received starting instructions from the conductor, then controlled the speed and braking of the locomotive throughout the journey. The engineer also monitored gauges and meters and kept the appropriate amount of water flowing into the boiler. Engineers were required to be highly skilled, as trains react differently to acceleration, braking, and negotiation of curves depending on the number of cars, slack in the train, loading, and condition of the rail. Before being entrusted with a train, engineers are required to serve as apprentices, moving cars and other rolling stock around the railyard to learn the trade. In the 1870s, an engineer would earn $3.25 per day on the Santa Fe Railway.

The fireman rode in the locomotive with the engineer, monitoring instruments and watching for track obstructions. They also shoveled coal into the engine firebox. The brakemen coupled and uncoupled cars and helped control the speed of the train with handbrakes, wheels located on the top of the cars, which were turned using a "brakeman's club." This was a dangerous job as it involved climbing from car to car,

and in 1893, the Federal Safety Appliance Act set standards for steps, ladders, running boards, and grab irons. One brakeman rode with the engineer and the other, the rear brakeman, rode in the caboose with the conductor. Now that airbrakes have replaced handbrakes, and the brakes are lower and do not require the brakeman's club, the job is safer and often only one brakeman is required, but the standards are still in place. Brakemen could expect a salary of $45 a month in the late nineteenth century.

CHAPTER FIVE

Track

Types of Lines

Deciding on railroad routes was a railroad company's most difficult task; profitability depended on the route, yet it could not be known where centers of commerce would emerge. Many railroad lines were built, only to be abandoned and dismantled. Active lines and vestiges of lines that are long gone can be seen everywhere in New Mexico: they run adjacent to major highways, branch off to important industrial companies, run in parallel arrays in busy railyards, and can be seen on both sides of rural railroad depots, even those that have been long out of service.

In addition to main lines, which link large cities and important destinations, railroad companies operate a variety of other lines. Branch lines, sometimes called brush lines, constitute about a quarter of the routes in the United States but handle only a fraction of the freight. Their lighter traffic can be justified if they lead to important industrial centers. Those that were too costly to operate and maintain have been abandoned or dismantled. Many branch lines were built to reach stores of coal or timber—important resources for steam railroads. As materials were depleted or when the steam era faded, these lines were also terminated. Constructed to take advantage of the area's coal stores, the branch from Carrizozo to Capitan was dismantled in 1943. Logging branches off the Denver & Rio Grande's Chile Line ceased operations in the 1920s and 1930s.

Another type of secondary line is the spur, a short out-and-back line. Like branch lines, these were commonly built off main lines to reach natural resources needed for railroad operations, such as coal and timber, or to reach the state's gold, uranium, or potash mines. Many spurs are intended to be used for a short time only. The Denver & Rio Grande's lumber spurs near Tres Piedras were in operation for only four years in the late nineteenth century.

Sidings are sections that split off from the track for a certain distance and then meet up with it again. Sidings accommodate crew changes, provide storage of cars or equipment, or allow engineers to wait for faster trains to pass. Sidings are most commonly found in railyards; even small depots on lines with limited traffic may be trackbound, wedged between main lines and active sidings. The primary track is often easy to spot; it is visible from the depot's bay window, while the siding is at the rear of the building, often the streetside.

Busy yards, which mostly occur at division points like Clovis, usually have many parallel tracks, called classification tracks, to allow for uncoupling and recoupling of cars to reconfigure trains. The classification track system is used to switch freight cars and arrange them according to their types, contents, and destinations.

Where trains needed to be moved from one line to another, for example, from a main line to a branch or onto a siding, a turnout is employed. A turnout diverts the wheels of a train from one track to another using a switch. Where the wheels cross the opposite rail, an X-shaped assembly called a *frog* is provided to allow the flange to pass. A wye is an arrangement of track and switches that allows a locomotive to perform a three-point turn and to face the opposite direction. Wyes are often employed at the end of a line.

Track Configuration

The basic rules for laying track have not changed since the inception of the railroad. The easiest track to build and maintain are runs that are both straight (called "tangent" by civil engineers) and level. But curves and grade changes are inevitable in a variable terrain.

Although curves are usually expressed in terms of the radius of a circle, measured in degrees, this is not practical for railroad curves. While a tight curve may be easy to lay out by locating the center of a circle and running a string of a certain length, the circle's radius, the gentle curvature required by trains have radii that are hundreds to thousands of feet long; the center of the circle would be impractically far away and the string would be too long. Therefore, train curvature is expressed in degrees rather than in radii. The degree of curvature is the angle through which the track turns in 100 feet.

With such a long length and having to adhere to track, trains cannot make sharp turns, so the absolute maximum for both standard- and narrow-gauge lines is thirty degrees (which corresponds to a radius of 193 feet). Main lines typically use curves of about one to two degrees, with a maximum of ten degrees. The gentle curve is crucial because these curves also have a corresponding safe maximum speed. At one degree, or a radius of 5,729 feet, a train can safely travel at no more than one hundred miles per hour, a speed reserved for freight shipments in the United States. Mountainous routes utilize curves of five to ten degrees, which would have corresponding radii of 1,146 feet and 573 feet. But the speed of a ten-degree curve is only thirty miles per hour, unacceptable on a high-speed main freight line. For comparison, the turning radius of cars and trucks is around 17 to 25 feet.

Grades also have an effect on train speed and function. The typical maximum design grade on main lines is 3 percent, but mountainous branch lines, such as the Cloud-Climbing Railroad to Cloudcroft, were as steep as 9 percent. These steep lines were served by low-speed locomotives that could travel only ten to twelve miles per hour, about the speed of the early prototype locomotives. In the mountains, steep grades often coexist with sharp curves, which is why a narrower track gauge, or spacing, was often employed on these routes. On main lines, curves are often compensated by reducing grades.

Raising the outer rail of a track, called super-elevation, is also used to compensate for the centrifugal force around curves. Super-elevation, also called banking, tips cars inward to keep them, literally, on track. The maximum banking used on a standard-gauge line is a 6-inch difference in elevation between the two rails, known as 6-inch cross-level.

Track gauge, the distance between the inside of the railheads, is another important aspect of the layout of lines. Track gauge was standardized to 4 feet, 8½ inches in 1863, when President Lincoln designated it as the gauge of the transcontinental railroad to be built to the Pacific. This was the standard used by the early railroad inventors, George Stephenson and his son Robert, and was chosen as the gauge used throughout Europe except in Spain, Portugal, Ireland, Finland, and Russia. The choice can be traced to the standard 4-foot, 9-inch dimension used by English tramways before the locomotive was invented, which, in turn, is attributed to the cart wheel spacing inferred from the 5-foot-wide Roman stone gateways.

Until President Lincoln made his determination, however, track gauge varied widely in the United States. Railroads south of the Potomac and Ohio rivers were mostly 5-foot-gauge until 1887, when several changed to standard over a single week to avoid

Fig. 7. Track structure. Photo by author.

switching cars and transferring loads. Some mountain railroads continued to be built of a smaller gauge to negotiate sharp curves and grades. These "narrow-gauge" railroads were less common, and rail spacing varied. The first narrow-gauge railroad, at 3 feet, was the Denver & Rio Grande, which traversed the narrow, winding, and steep passes of Colorado and northern New Mexico.

Gauge allows for a ¾-inch clearance between the wheel flanges and the railheads in order to accommodate some shifting of rails and wear in service.

Track Structure

A railroad could still function without dedicated buildings for ticketing, but not without the track. In the early years railroad companies focused on track mileage, the crucial component of the system, at the expense of depots and other structures. The track still receives the bulk of a railroad company's funds, exceeding buildings or even locomotives. The basic components of the track structure are the rail, crossties, tie plates, rail anchors, and ballast. The pur-

pose of this system is to distribute the concentrated weight of the train—locomotives, cars, and cargo—from the rail to the ground below.

The word *track* is often used as a synonym for *rail*, but the rail is actually just one component of the track composition. The function of rails is to guide the wheels of the locomotives and train cars. Early rails were constructed of cast iron, first produced around 1794. With its high carbon content, cast iron is hard but very brittle and was often damaged by the weight of locomotives. Wrought iron, almost pure iron with a very low carbon content, was then introduced, but while this alloy was corrosion resistant, strong, and malleable, it was too soft and did not wear well. Fortunately, the mid-nineteenth century, which saw the development of railroad systems, also saw the development of economical processes for converting iron into steel. Steel, an alloy with a small amount of carbon and mechanical properties that could be adjusted, was ideal for railroad use, and was now much less expensive. Steel rail may last as long as sixty years before it must be scrapped. To extend the wear of steel rails, new rail is laid on main lines, while branch lines are laid with "relay" rail that has already served several years on a main line.

Rails are generally 6 to 8 inches high but vary in weight. Small coal mines once used track weighing as little as 12 pounds per yard. Heavy-duty main-line track weighs about 126 pounds per yard. Most rail now produced weighs between 112 and 145 pounds per yard. Rail is still produced in traditional 39-foot lengths, which was the longest that could fit on 40-foot railroad cars for distribution. Newer "ribbon" rail, continuous-welded track a quarter mile long, has fewer joints, creating a smoother ride and reduced track and car maintenance.

The rails distribute the weight of the train to the ground below through the wood crossties, often called sleepers. If the rail was placed directly on the ties, the wood could be crushed or cut by the rail itself. So the weight of the rails is distributed to the ties by tie plates, which extend the life of the ties and provide additional rail stability. Tie plates are essentially a bearing surface and can be as long as 18 inches in lines with heavy traffic.

Crossties are typically made of hardwood, 9 inches by 7 inches by 8½ feet long for a standard-gauge railway, and are spaced 21 inches apart, although very early railroads used various sizes of ties based on the availability of wood and the expected level of use of the railroad. Other early railroads, in an effort to improve durability, mounted rails to stone blocks embedded in the ground. Not only was this expensive, the friction between the rail and the stone damaged both the rail and the train. The stone was also prone to shifting, which put the railroad out of gauge. Wood ties, however, are ideal. They hold the rails in gauge, distribute weight well, and provide flexibility and cushioning. They are also much less expensive than the stone alternative.

The primary problem with wood ties is their tendency to rot, which was addressed with the use of creosote, a gas-tar preservative first used on railroad crossties in 1839. Railroads charted the performance of ties and kept service records by driving date nails into the ends of ties; if a rotted or damaged tie was removed, the date on the nail was noted. Ties were never removed due to age, so the nails did not indicate when to replace ties. The embossed or raised numbers on the head signify either the year of preservative treatment, if the nail was driven into the tie at the treatment plant, or the year the tie was laid, if it was driven in at the track. As the

use of creosote, which is now pressure impregnated into ties, became widespread, it was clear that ties needed replacement less frequently, and date nails were phased out. They were used by the Santa Fe Railway only from 1901 through 1969, but can still be seen on the ties in many old lines. They are 2½ inches long with ¼-inch shanks. The shape of the head can be round, square, diamond-shaped, or pentagonal; the head shape was often a railroad company's code for the type of treatment of the tie. Some railroads now use concrete ties, a much more recent development that address the problems of the old stone ties while retaining the qualities of the wood and eliminating the possibility of rot.

Tie plates are attached to the crossties with track spikes. Extra holes in the plates are used for respiking or for placing additional spikes to provide stability on sharp curves. Most spikes used on main and branch lines have a 6-inch long, ⅝-inch square shaft. Early logging and mining railroads and some narrow-gauge railways often used shorter, smaller spikes. Their size was not due to the smaller wheel spacing, a common misconception, but rather was a factor of the temporary nature of many narrow-gauge railroads, which were intended only to serve for a limited number of years until the natural resources were depleted.

One problem with railroad track composition was "creep," the tendency for rails to "run" or move in the direction of travel. This condition is most pronounced with temperature changes, steep grades, and loaded trains braking in only one direction, which forces ties and switches out of line and develops stresses that make track buckle sideways. Rail anchors, also called anti-creepers, are spring clips that snap onto the base of the rail and push against the tie to restrain motion. There are several types of rail anchors, but the most common is the drive-on type, which was first patented in the early 1900s. In one configuration, the rail anchor looks much like a heavy-duty, three-dimensional paperclip, with one end looped through a receptacle in the tie plate.

The base of the track structure is ballast, which holds crossties in place and spreads out the load to the adjacent ground. Ballast depth is dependent on the soil conditions and can extend anywhere from 6 inches to 30 inches below the crossties. As the heaviest component of the track structure, ballast must be easily available within reasonable hauling distances. Although crushed rock or slags are structurally superior, other materials have been used because they are local, including cinders, oyster shells, and coarse sand. Almost any material sufficed because the key to successful ballast is adequate drainage. As a result, in level country such as much of New Mexico, track is laid on a low embankment with side ditches; many of the state's abandoned railroad grades now consist of this telltale bump in the terrain.

Fig. 8. Date nail from Santa Fe Railway, 1928. Photo by author.

CHAPTER SIX

Rolling Stock

The essence of a railroad are its wheeled engines and cars, the rolling stock. It is the locomotives, maintenance of way cars, freight cars, and passenger cars that captivate "trainspotters" and delight small children, who can explain in detail the difference between hoppers and gondolas or tank engines and diesel-electric locomotives.

Locomotives

A train is defined as one or more engines coupled together, with or without cars. In other words, without the locomotive, there is no train. The locomotive, which provides the power and therefore motion, has evolved more than any other part of the railroad. The earliest locomotives were wood-fueled steam engines, but by the mid-1800s, and for most of the era of steam, coal was the fuel of choice. Early coal-fired engines had a coal-tender capacity of about fourteen tons and a water-storage capacity of about ten thousand gallons. Later engines could carry up to twenty-five tons and twenty thousand gallons. One pound of coal turned six pounds (seven-tenths of a gallon) of water to steam, so the railroad required far more water than coal. But because water was more readily available, locomotive storage capacities were based on two water stops to one fuel stop. The water was often carried in a separate tank pulled directly behind the locomotive, which led to the name "tank engine."

Steam locomotives were generally of five types:

switchers, used for yard duties; short-haul locomotives, which carried both freight and passengers; long-haul freight engines; passenger locomotives; and gear-driven locomotives for low-speed logging and mining operations.

Steam locomotives are designated by their wheel configuration, which is expressed using the Whyte Coding System, developed around 1900 by Frederick M. Whyte. The first number in the classification refers to the number of "leading truck" wheels, also called forward guide wheels or bogies, which helped steer the locomotive through curves. The second number refers to the number of "drive wheels" that provided the traction force for pulling. The last number refers to the number of "trailing truck" wheels, also called bogies, which supported the locomotive and provided guidance while backing up. Therefore, a 2-8-0 had two leading truck wheels, eight drivers, and no trailing truck wheels.

Through the years, the weight, hauling capacity, and speed of steam locomotives increased steadily. In 1879, when the Santa Fe Railway first entered New Mexico, steam locomotives weighed about thirty-six and a half tons. Sixty years later, they weighed seventy-five tons. The last generation of steam engines, developed in the 1940s, burned fuel oil rather than coal, and their weight rose dramatically to ninety-nine tons.

The use of fuel oil was short-lived. Diesel-electric locomotives using internal-combustion engines were much more fuel efficient than the external-combustion steam locomotive. Diesel was named for Rudolph Diesel, who invented an engine that ran on a mixture of compressed air and oil. The diesel-electric engine turns an alternator or generator, which then produces electricity to power traction motors connected to the locomotive's axles. The diesels were not only more fuel efficient, they also eliminated the need for coal, which was becoming increasingly more expensive. They also required a smaller train crew, allowed for better speed control with dynamic braking, decreased maintenance costs, and enabled higher speeds on curves due to a lower center of gravity.

The first commercial diesel-electric locomotive was invented by General Electric in 1918 for a New York railroad. In 1924, General Electric teamed with American Locomotive Company (ALCO) to market diesel-electric yard switchers. The yard switchers were successful, but diesel engines were not used in long-run, high-speed service until 1934, when the Chicago, Burlington & Quincy, more commonly called the Burlington Route, introduced its Zephyrs, sleek stainless-steel, streamlined passenger engines.

The Santa Fe Railway, which always had difficulty obtaining coal and water on its western lines, adopted the new technology quickly, acquiring its first true diesel locomotive in 1935, a six-hundred-horsepower yard switcher called #2300. By 1938, the railroad operated ten new streamliner passenger trains powered by yellow and red diesels. The sleek "warbonnet" paint scheme, first introduced on those diesel engines, became an integral part of the railroad's image. The railroad also ordered the first freight diesels in the United States, painting these blue and yellow in the same style. The Santa Fe soon owned the largest diesel fleet in the world.

Diesels sometimes use a modification of the Whyte Coding System to clarify how many axles the engine has. For example, a 6-0-6 would have six front wheels (and, therefore, three axles) and six rear wheels. Diesel locomotives almost never have a center truck if they have both front and rear trucks. But diesels also have their own more complicated designation system.

The early diesels were elegant, futuristic, and well designed. But the end of the steam era had consequences for western communities. The diesel engines bypassed former water stops, so remote stations that existed primarily to provide water and fuel to the train were no longer needed. Many towns died as a result, signaling the end of the romantic era of railroading. The second generation of diesels, which were developed after 1950, lacked the streamlining of their predecessors. The utilitarian engines included General Motors' general-purpose diesels, called Geeps, used on branch lines, for switching, and for some passenger runs.

Passenger Cars

Passenger trains were the pride of a railroad's system, with luxurious interiors and fine food. Whether made up of all passenger cars (known as Pullman cars) or with freight towed in the rear, they were the focus of a railroad's design efforts and marketing attention. New Mexico's passenger trains included the California Limited, the Santa Fe's premier passenger train from Chicago to California. The daily train began its run in 1892. A weekly, extra-fare, all-Pullman train was added in 1911. Called the DeLuxe, it made the Chicago to Los Angeles run in sixty-three hours. It was replaced by the Chief in 1926.

As the streamliners took over in the 1930s, the weekly Super Chief provided the passenger service. The streamliners, made of stainless steel, weighed almost forty-two tons rather than the eight tons of standard passenger cars, but pulled by the new, efficient engines, the train set a record, making the weekly run in only thirty-seven hours. The last run of the Super Chief was on May 13, 1968. When Amtrak began providing all passenger service in the United States in the 1970s, they borrowed the trains' romantic names for their less lavish Pullmans and retained the name of the Super

Chief with permission from the Santa Fe.

During the first half of the twentieth century, following the development of gas-powered internal-combustion engines, another type of passenger train was developed for branch lines with low ridership. The doodlebug, named for its insect-like appearance, was a cross between a locomotive and a passenger car, with an internal-combustion engine in the front section and a passenger compartment in the rear. If needed, the rear portion could be used for baggage and freight, and the doodlebug could pull a passenger car, but most were run as single units, usually hauling passengers but sometimes hauling only mail and freight. The result was a cost-effective train that could be operated with only a two-person crew, and by the 1930s, they were very successful. The 1958 Transportation Act, which limited state power over rail passenger service, coupled with the low profit potential of short-run passenger routes, caused railroads to cancel their branch-line passenger trains, and doodlebugs were made obsolete.

Freight Cars

Less than 5 percent of railroad revenue in the United States comes from passenger service. The majority of the cars seen today are freight cars, which have become quite specialized in response to the requirements of the cargo they carry. There are six basic types of freight car: boxcars, refrigerator cars, flatcars, gondolas, hoppers, and tank cars. The "consist" of a freight train is its makeup by types of cars and their contents, usually a mixture of several types of cars.

The enclosed boxcars have sliding center doors to permit loading and unloading of packaged or palletized items. A more flexible "combination door" boxcar has grain doors across its regular doors so that it can handle either packages or granular bulk commodities.

Grain mill products are sometimes shipped in food service boxcars with seamless plastic linings to prevent contamination. Specialized boxcars have been developed for more sensitive cargo such as newsprint rolls (which tend to shift and flatten without restraint) and fragile stone, glass, and clay products, which are denoted on the boxcar doors with the letters "DF" for "damage free." Auto carriers, or trilevel racks of automobiles, represent an evolution of the boxcar. Though they were once open, they have been enclosed to prevent vandalism and theft.

Refrigerator cars, once called reefers, are a type of boxcar used to keep perishable food items cold in transit; they were first put into service in 1851 on the Northern Railroad of New York. Early reefer cars were made of wood, with ice bunkers built into the end of each car, and insulated with felt, hair, or sawdust. The ice bunkers were filled not only with ice inserted through hatches on the roof but also with salt to lower the melting point and therefore the temperature of the ice. Refilling occurred about every 250 to 400 miles from icehouses at regular railroad stops. Mechanical refrigeration was introduced in a few trains in the 1920s and extensively in trucks in the 1930s. But because the refrigeration used in trains was powered by the axles of the car, supplemental units had to be provided to keep the load cool when the train came to a stop, and railroads were slow to adopt the technology. When self-contained gas or diesel refrigeration units were developed in the late 1940s, railroad companies began to see the benefits, including the smaller size of the units compared to ice bunkers, which allowed for a larger payload. Now, in addition to mechanically refrigerated cars, railroads also use insulated refrigerated cars, which can maintain temperatures safe for many food products without a mechanical cooling system.

Flatcars have been common since the early days of railroading. The versatile cars traditionally carried lumber and wood products for sale or for railroad use. Lumber is still hauled on flatcars, allowing for easy loading and unloading by forklift, but most flatcars carry trailers or containers. Trailers can be offloaded and quickly transferred to waiting trucks, and containers, often stacked two high, are transferred from ships and riverboats. Intermodal containers are now the largest segment of traffic on the Burlington Northern Santa Fe's Chicago to California corridor, and the volume of traffic grows each year.

The high sides and solid bottoms of gondolas make them ideal for items that are best loaded and unloaded by crane. Loads carried by gondola include stone, waste or scrap materials, and sometimes coal (depending on unloading facilities). Gondolas with removable covers allow metal products to be protected from the weather but still unloaded by gantry cranes.

Hoppers are cars with hinged trapdoors and inclined floors that use a bottom-dump system for fast unloading. They come in specialized sizes for carrying materials of varying densities, including small hoppers for very dense metallic ores; medium-size "aggregate" hoppers for stone, gravel, and sand; large-capacity hoppers to carry coke the short distances from coking plants to steel mills; and very large hoppers to carry woodchips to paper plants. Hoppers rather than gondolas are also used to carry coal where the unloading destination requires a bottom-dump configuration. Some hoppers are covered to carry grain or nonmetallic minerals such as salt or phosphate, which require protection from the weather.

Railroads once employed tank cars for a variety of loads, but they are now used mostly to carry chemicals. Because many chemicals require specialized linings, most tank cars carry only one class of product. For example, liquified petroleum, or LP, the form of petroleum commonly transported by train, is shipped only in petroleum tank cars.

Maintenance of Way

Maintenance of way cars often look like tractors on tracks. The equipment includes the miscellaneous cars that are needed to keep the railroad in working order, from cranes to track maintenance vehicles to snow-removal equipment to railcar movers.

Cabooses

The function of the caboose was to provide a vantage point for the conductor and the rear brakeman from which they could view the train and conduct their work. The cars were called a variety of names including cabin cars, waycars, shacks, and, in New Mexico, crummies; the term *caboose* was originally a nautical term for a cooking galley. The first caboose, a simple boxcar used at the end of a train on the Auburn & Syracuse Railroad in the 1840s, was exactly that: a place where the conductor had a desk and ate his meals. The cupolas that extend from the top of cabooses provided a better view of the train; later trains employed bay windows on the sides of the car for the same purpose. Most cabooses included seats, a stove for cooking and heating, bunks for the crew, cupboards for storage, and a desk for the conductor. As train operations evolved, the need for a rear observation platform was eliminated. Now EOT (end of train) monitors are placed on the last car, and cabooses are used only where backup movements warrant their use.

CHAPTER SEVEN

Railroad Depots

A New Building Type

The first railroad stops were, like stagecoach stops, in hotels and general stores where passengers could buy tickets and wait for arriving trains. Passenger service, however, was only a small percentage of railroad operations. A new building type would soon emerge, providing a hub to accommodate passenger, freight, and management operations. These early depots were relatively utilitarian, but when stations began to be seen as the public face of the railroad company, plans became more elaborate. And each station was also gateway to the town it served, so it was designed to represent not only the railroad company but also the community.

First Impressions

With competing railroads and a high volume of passenger traffic in the eastern United States, a first impression was important to financial success. The grand terminal stations in the East were intended to impress. But in the West the low volume of traffic did not warrant large stations. Funds were better spent on track, bridges, and tunnels to traverse the difficult terrain. Since more stations were required to cover the large distances between cities, they needed to be cost effective and functional. An architect was rarely employed in depot design; engineers provided plans and they were used repeatedly, a first step toward increased standardization.

The familiar form of the rural depot evolved as a response to operational, passenger, and freight needs. With few trains each day and a much lower volume of freight than in large cities, a single main track on one side of the depot was all that was required. Other track configurations were rarely used, and trainsheds were unnecessary. This led to an elongated rectangle depot shape with its long side parallel to the tracks and the functions inside arranged so that each had track access. A projecting trackside window gave the station agent a better view of the trains along the track. And the overhanging eaves sheltered passengers on the platform from sun or rain. Brackets supported the deep overhang structurally. The style grew out of practical concerns to become the small-town railroad depot so easily recognizable today.

Depot Layout

Railroad depots were the focal points of railroad operations. Although some depots served only passengers, and others existed solely to move freight, "combination depots," which provided space for both functions, were more common in the West. From a single location, the railroad company could coordinate train movements, attend to passengers, and move freight.

The combination depot had a familiar layout. At the heart of the building was the ticket office or agent's bay, named for its bay window, which provided an expanded view of the tracks. In large cities, this office was used by a telegrapher and a station agent, but in small cities and towns, the station agent worked alone, coordinating train movements by acting as a link between the dispatch center and train crew. The agent communicated with the dispatch center via telegraph, then distributed the dispatcher's train orders to train crews as they passed, in turn

Fig. 9. Baggage cart, Cumbres & Toltec
Scenic Railroad, ca. 1996.
Photo by author.

informing dispatch of train movements. Before train orders, railroad engineers adhered to a timetable, but it did not allow for minute adjustments or unforeseen conditions. Train orders were instructions to vary from the timetable, a potentially dangerous but necessary procedure. Although at first received only at division-point stops, the first en route train order was given by Superintendent Charles Minot of the Erie Railroad in 1851 to change the meeting point between two trains. The timetable and train order method of coordinating train movements was quickly adopted and was used until the mid-1940s.

The telegraph allowed for the communications crucial to issuing train orders. Samuel Morse invented the electromagnetic telegraph in 1836 as well as the code for transmitting letters of the alphabet via electrical pulses. The Baltimore & Ohio first tested telegraphy on the railroad in 1844, and soon railroads strung telegraph wires in tandem with the construction of new lines. The original Morse code was

slightly modified for railroad work.

After a telegraphed message from dispatch, the station agent wrote the train orders on a thin paper called onionskin and copied them using carbon paper. A minimum of six copies were necessary to supply the five-person train crew and allow for a copy for station records. The agent notified the crew that there were train orders by shifting the indicators on the semaphore, a signaling apparatus outside the agent's bay. Since the train did not stop at every station and could not stop just to receive orders, the agent placed the papers in a wire holder fastened to a bamboo hoop with a long handle. The entire hoop was handed up to the engineer and another to the conductor in the caboose; they extended their arms through the hoops, took the orders, and then discarded the hoops to be used again.

Although the telegraph was still the main instrument for sending messages of record, by the 1940s train orders were received by telephone. Soon after, the use of centralized traffic control (CTC), first used

Fig. 10. Sliding freight-room door hardware, Rincon depot, ca. 1996. Photo by author.

the agent and into storage to await the train. Agents handled all manner of freight as well, from livestock to ore; the freight room was on the other side of the baggage room but still close to the agent. The type and amount of freight determined the size of freight rooms and also the need for a raised platform. Freight rooms at boxcar level allowed freight to be moved onto small carts of the same height for direct transfer; most also were open to both the trackside and the streetside to load large items into the freight room and then onto the train. To discourage vandalism and theft, freight rooms were utilitarian areas, with only a few small high windows and unpainted wood walls. They can also be the most interesting rooms in a depot, with the agent's scale still in working order in many depots such as Lamy, and large, sliding doors with ornate hardware. It was in the freight rooms that station agents traditionally signed their names and dates of service, captivating graffiti from another era.

Construction

There are several basic depot construction types. Depots constructed of wood frame were versatile and could be easily moved to new locations as needed. Before 1900 they were placed on wooden piles for stability, but after 1900 concrete and concrete block footings were used. The exterior of the frame depots was usually board and batten but sometimes clapboard. Beaded paneling on the interior and wood shingles on the roof made for a highly flammable structure, at risk from sparks thrown from passing trains. When a station served an established town or the town's population increased, a safer and more permanent and imposing structure made of brick or concrete was warranted.

Coal- or wood-burning stoves heated early depots. Stoves in the waiting room and the agent's

by the Chicago, Burlington & Quincy Railroad in 1927, became widespread. Since dispatchers could remotely control switches, the timetable and train order system was made obsolete.

In addition to providing instructions to the train crew, the station agent also kept the books and maintained the station. The agent also announced departures and arrivals and sold tickets to passengers, which is why the agent's bay is sometimes called the ticket office and why it was adjacent to passenger waiting rooms. In small stations, there was only one waiting room, but at larger stops, men and women were separated. Early depots employed outhouses, but soon restrooms could be found at important stops; they were later added in most depots. A typical layout borrowed space from the agent's bay to create restrooms on the streetside opposite the bay.

Since the agent also handled baggage, the baggage room was on the other side of the agent's bay, and bags could be transferred directly from the waiting room to bay often used the same chimney, connecting directly to the flue with a stovepipe. Although gas heaters were installed from the 1930s (though not in many New Mexican depots until the 1950s), the holes where the pipes met the wall can still be seen, a clue to the location of the original stoves.

Kerosene lamps provided night lighting in early depots. These were replaced by incandescent gas lamps in which a gas flame heated a finely woven mesh mantle to produce a brighter light. Electricity was common in nonrailroad buildings in the 1880s but was not used until the 1920s in New Mexico's depots.

CHAPTER EIGHT

Unique Aspects of New Mexico's Depots

In Europe and in the eastern part of the United States, towns were already established before railroad stations were built, so the depot often stood apart both architecturally and geographically. Towers and iron arches were popular. Dramatic, long-span train-sheds and elaborate track systems were sensible solutions to accommodating large numbers of passengers. In the West, though, future traffic could not be predicted, and the economic reality of needing more miles of track and roadbed to reach a destination meant that money was spent on infrastructure, not buildings. Although depots were needed every ten to thirty miles on the line, many of these were simple boxcar depots. Where a town was expected to develop, a small wood depot of a standard plan and materials was erected with the anticipation that if the community developed sufficiently, the frame depot could be replaced with something grander. In these cases, the previous frame depots were used as freight depots or moved to other locations.

Although New Mexico's depots shared characteristics with other depots in the country, its structures developed a distinct regional character in response to the open spaces of the Southwest, the scattered population, and New Mexico's unique culture. The hallmarks of New Mexico's depots include standardized plans, the ability to be moved as needed, space for the station agent and

his family and, as the railroads became more established, the use of a new regional railroad style.

Standardization

In the early years of New Mexico railroading, the style of the territory's depots was usually a company standard design. This standardization of railroad depot design coincided with standardization in daily life. Brand-names like Singer sewing machines, Quaker oats, and Ivory soap were emerging. Items that were previously built to order, including building components like millwork, were available from sources such as the Sears and Roebuck catalog (which began its mail-order business in 1886) and the Montgomery Ward catalog.

Standardization was embraced by railroad companies. Premanufactured items included components of rolling stock, couplers used to link cars together, and signals that warned of approaching trains. It was a natural step for major railroad lines to introduce standard plans and building elevations that were not only inexpensive to produce but also presented a corporate image. The Santa Fe first introduced standards for entire buildings rather than just parts in 1910. The "Frame Depot No. 2 for Branch Lines," among other plans, was used extensively in the West. The small 24-foot by 48-foot depot had a simple layout: a single waiting room on one end, a freight room on the other end, and an office in the center. Restrooms were located outside, "to be located where most convenient and least objectionable," according to the standards.[1] The semioctagonal agent's bay projected 3½ feet and the platform was to be 300 feet long.

Paint colors were also standardized. Early New Mexican stations were painted a deep red called mineral brown, with bronze-green and white trim. The red was later changed to a lighter golden yellow, perhaps because the hot, steady sun had a tendency to blister paint; this was the color that people in the West associated with the Santa Fe. Standardization of railroad buildings was very apparent in the West, where unique railroad structures, reserved for large towns, were rare.

Mobility

Another feature of early depots in New Mexico was their mobility. Population shifts in the West were common. Towns grew and then faded rapidly, influenced by factors such as the opening and closing of mines, inexpensive land that enticed settlement, and droughts that drove settlers away. The beauty of wood-frame depots was that they were easily transported on flatcars and relocated as needed.

Many wood-frame depots served several towns before they were retired. A 16-foot by 40-foot depot was built in Lucy along the Belen Cutoff line in 1908. This was relocated to Estancia on the New Mexico Central branch in 1951, and when the depot was retired it was moved to a ranch south of town. Another depot was constructed in Torrance, moved to Corona, and then sold by the railroad to private owners who relocated it to Alamogordo. It is now used as a model-railroad museum.

Because they were so portable, a railroad's wood-frame depots survived the cost-cutting measures employed after the decline of the railroads. Instead of destroying the structures, the companies sold them to communities or private individuals, who easily hauled them away.

Living Quarters

Many New Mexico towns lacked acceptable housing for the station agent, a problem that was magnified if the station agent had a family. For this reason, railroad companies sometimes incorporated living quarters into their standard plans, usually in the form of second stories, which elevated the apartment above dangerous tracks.

The Southern Pacific was partial to including living quarters, and one of its most widely used plans was the Standard No. 22. Although once ubiquitous, the only example left in New Mexico is the depot in Columbus. The Santa Fe Railway incorporated housing into its Eastern Railway of New Mexico depots, which featured second-story apartments with a living room, kitchen, and two bedrooms or a dormitory-like configuration of two rooms and two bathrooms.

After World War II, when rationing of gas and rubber had ended and the popularity and availability of automobiles increased, the station agent no longer needed to live so near the depot. Since property taxes on the buildings were based on square footage, railroad companies removed the second stories of many wood-frame depots. Their operating costs were reduced, but an important historical feature was lost.

Wide-Ranging Styles

When the size or importance of cities warranted something grander than a standard wood-frame structure, the style chosen in New Mexico varied. Eastern Brick depots were common on the east coast but rare in New Mexico; even when the style was used, the designs tended to incorporate regional or Mission-style elements. The brick depot in Las Vegas has Mission features such as wrought-iron roof brackets and a quatrefoil detail on a parapet in addition to the more standard dormer windows. The Denver & Rio Grande/New Mexico Central depot in Santa Fe was a simplified version of the somewhat grander eastern depots. Many of the attractive brick detailing that was

Fig. 11. Las Vegas depot, ca. 1910. Courtesy of the Museum of New Mexico, neg. no. 35877.

a hallmark of these depots was later covered in stucco to approximate a southwestern style when a more regional look was preferred. Las Vegas's handsome brick was until recently coated in stucco.

The style most associated with railroad depots in the Southwest is the Mission Revival style. Among the first people to recognize the unique and marketable design features of the California missions was Charles Fletcher Lummis, editor of the *Land of Sunshine*, subtitled "A Magazine of California and the Southwest," founded in 1894. His romanticized version of Spanish colonial California was featured in the magazine. The elegant and eclectic Spanish-influenced buildings of the 1915 Panama-California Exposition in San Diego, which celebrated the completion of the Panama Canal, established

the popularity of what was to be called Mission Revival style. The style borrowed elements from the missions such as the use of stucco, tile roofs, arched openings, projecting parapets—called *remates*—with curved edges, and quatrefoil windows. Mission Revival combined these features with square towers and hipped roofs that were a signature of the Italian Villa style popular in California after the Civil War. The style was sometimes criticized as derivative and sentimental, but as Lummis commented, "The missions are . . . the best capital southern California has."[2] In his opinion, the Southwest was "exclusively the romantic corner of the United States as well as the wonderland of the continent."[3]

The first Mission Revival depot was the San Pedro, Los Angeles & Salt Lake Railroad station built

Fig. 12. Commerce and Industries Building, Panama-California Exposition, 2003. Photo by author.

in Riverside, California, now referred to as the Union Pacific depot, for the railroad that acquired the line in 1921. Although it was the first Mission Revival depot, Riverside has the typical curved parapeted ends, rectangular towers, arched openings, and hipped and gabled roofs used later.

The features of Mission Revival were well suited to depots. Arches, arcades, and large overhangs provided shelter, simple designs were inexpensive to build, and masonry walls were fireproof, an advantage considering that sparks thrown from passing trains regularly caused wooden depots to burn. Remates, ornamental false fronts that projected above the roofline, visually heightened depot buildings and made them appear more solid and imposing. The use of the style was symbiotic, however, as the railroads played an important role in the development and public acceptance of Mission Revival.

In most of the West, the railroads favored a simplified, abstracted version of Mission Revival style. The tall chimneys of Eastern Brick–style depots and exposed, profiled roof brackets were common carry-

overs; both can be seen in Santa Fe's depots in Las Cruces and Portales. The Santa Fe Railway used the style even on smaller depots, to establish a corporate identity. Where Mission Revival structures would have quatrefoil ornaments, such as the tops of curved parapets, the Santa Fe embedded their familiar cross and circle logo in the stucco facade. The Fred Harvey Company, associated with the Santa Fe, used the style in its dining rooms, lunchrooms, and hotels. Mission Revival Harvey Houses at Belen, Albuquerque, Lamy, and other cities complemented the exotic train journey through the Southwest and promoted tourism. The only other railroad to build a Mission Revival depot in New Mexico was the Rock Island.

The Santa Fe Railway also experimented with a Pueblo Revival style, which capitalized on both American Indian and Spanish design that already existed in New Mexico. The simple forms and parapeted flat roofs recall historic buildings such as Santa Fe's Palace of the Governors, the first colonial capital and oldest European structure in Santa Fe. Mary Colter, the Fred Harvey Company's staff architect, thoroughly researched Spanish and American Indian building traditions for commissions such as the Gallup depot and the attached El Navajo Hotel.

CHAPTER NINE

Other Railroad Structures

In addition to the depots, a railroad's public face, building types developed to serve the new industry's needs. Railroad buildings can be classified in three broad categories: those for the movement of goods, those for the movement of passengers, those for the service of the railroad, and those for railroad workers. In small towns, railroad depots sometimes served all functions, but in larger railyards, structures with more specific uses were required. Car-repair sheds, drop pits, engine-washing platforms, icehouses, machine shops, mail cranes, pump houses, sand houses, oil houses, storehouses, roundhouses, turntables, water tanks, watchman's towers, bunkhouses, and section houses filled railyards, and hotels, restaurants, warehouses, and factories clustered around the depot.

Movement of Goods

Freight Depots

Where a large amount of freight was expected, in the important trade center of Santa Fe, for example, freight depots handled shipping separately from passengers. Many freight depots were formerly wood-frame passenger depots that were converted to freight uses when the growth of a city justified a more imposing facility. Therefore, freight buildings often look much like combination depots.

Railway Express Agency

The important job of moving goods was supplemented by the Railway Express Agency, the precursor to today's express shipping companies such as the United Parcel Service. The federal government formed the company in 1918 when it merged the nation's major express carriers—Adams, American Express, Wells Fargo, and Southern Express—into a single public corporation called the American Railway Express Company. An association of railroads bought the company in 1929 and changed the name to Railway Express Agency, or REA. The baggage carts and green trucks with the red REA logo were a familiar sight around the United States. Although the company filed for bankruptcy in 1975, some historic REA shipping offices remain.

Movement of Passengers

Platforms and Parks

Although most western towns did not shelter passengers with elaborate trainsheds, a platform provided a walkable, yet uncovered, link between the depot and the train. Brick platforms were common, and the most common type of brick used in New Mexico was from Coffeyville, Kansas. Due to Coffeyville's abundant clay and hard-firing process, bricks from the area could withstand harsh freeze-and-thaw weather cycles. It was one of the largest centers of brick manufacturing at the turn of the century and at one time had eighteen different plants. In the 1900s, bricks paved not only railroad platforms but also streets and sidewalks, and the plants produced over 750,000 bricks per day at their peak to meet demand with three major railroad lines handling distribution. Many southwestern railroad platforms are still paved with the long-lasting bricks. One familiar logo that can be seen at many of New Mexico's depots is "Coffeyville VB&T Co.," the Coffeyville Vitrified Brick and Tile Company.

Adjacent to the platform, the railroad company sometimes provided a shady park where passengers could eat a picnic lunch while waiting for trains. The parks have not been maintained, but the vestiges of the welcoming green gardens can sometimes be seen.

Ticket Booths

Some railyards, particularly division points, provided separate ticket booths where passengers could buy tickets. The booths were small buildings located directly on the depot platform for passenger access. In New Mexico there were only a few ticket booths, including one on the bustling Clovis railyard; today none remain.

Hotels, Dining Rooms, and Lunchrooms

In addition to the railway depot, the railroad provided weary passengers with lunchrooms, dining rooms, and hotels. In the early days of rail travel, the train stopped for only twenty minutes; since there were no dining cars, passengers were forced to find food at local establishments. The twenty minutes was not enough time to find food and return to the train, however, and local restaurants were often of poor quality in any case. This problem was more pronounced in the West, where there were fewer provisions, smaller towns, and longer journeys.

An English entrepreneur, Fred Harvey, with experience in both the restaurant business and midwestern railroads, decided that there was profit to be made in providing railroad passengers with "good service and clean food." His longtime employer, the Burlington Northern, rejected his idea, but the Santa Fe Railway was immediately interested. In 1876, Harvey leased a portion of the Santa Fe's Topeka, Kansas, depot and

opened the first Harvey House lunch counter; it was the beginning of a successful partnership. His first hotel, in the important rail terminal of Florence, Kansas, opened the same year.

The Harvey system allowed for the twenty-minute stop by using the station agent as a liaison between the train and the manager of the Harvey House. As the train approached, the train crew telegraphed the number of customers for the lunch counter and dining room and even took orders so that food could be ready as the passengers arrived. The exotic menus, elegant buildings, and hardworking, wholesome "Harvey Girl" waitresses helped civilize the rugged West and raise the standard of dining establishments and accommodations.

As more lunchrooms, dining rooms, and hotels were launched, "Meals by Fred Harvey" became a Santa Fe Railway slogan. The railroad not only constructed the Harvey Houses, it also transported Harvey employees and supplies for free. Although dining-car service appeared on other lines as early as 1883, the Santa Fe operated no dining cars west of Kansas City until 1892, and in 1893, Fred Harvey was given the dining-car service as well. The Santa Fe Railway also benefited from the alliance. They earned an invaluable reputation for quality and service, and ridership increased.

The Harvey Houses were located trackside and, constructed by the railroad, were often similar in style to the depot next door. There were once nine Harvey lunch or dining rooms and eight hotels in New Mexico; several were among the grandest in the system. Harvey's house architect, Mary Colter, created a style for the buildings that combined Spanish and American Indian influences, including arched portales, wooden beams, adobe, and earth tones. New Mexico's surviving Harvey Houses include the Belen dining room, Las Vegas's Castanenda Hotel and the nearby Montezuma Hotel, Clovis's Gran Quivira Hotel, and the La Fonda in Santa Fe.

The symbiotic partnership between the Santa Fe Railroad and the Harvey Company outlived Fred Harvey, who died in 1901; his family carried on the tradition of quality restaurants and hotels and expanded into Fred Harvey's Indian Detours in 1925 to revive tourism, declining as a result of World War I. The Detours, another successful venture with the Santa Fe Railway, were conceived of and managed for the Harvey Company by Major R. Hunter Clarkson, whose father-in-law was the railroad's vice president. On August 25, 1925, he launched the new enterprise with these words: "There is more of historic, prehistoric, human and scenic interest . . . than in any similar area of the world, not excepting India, Egypt, Europe or Asia. . . . The big idea is not only to let people know what is in Northern New Mexico but to tell them what it is when they see it."[1] Indian Detours brought adventurous tourists from the train to remote areas of the Southwest in so-called Harveycars and Clarkson buses with southwestern-attired, knowledgeable guides. The irony of the new venture was that it inadvertently encouraged tourists to sightsee in their own cars, making both the train and the Detours obsolete.

Service of the Railroad

Centers of Operations

At the division-point operations centers, larger office buildings supplemented the ticket agent and telegrapher's office in the depot. These buildings provided offices for the division-point staff, including the superintendent, the trainmaster, the dispatcher, the roadmaster, the superintendent's clerks and secretaries, and the engineering department. In addition, file rooms and a drafting room for engineering were often included.

Repair and Maintenance

The most important activity at division points was the repair and maintenance of locomotives; steam locomotives in particular required constant upkeep. About twice a day, all parts and pipes were inspected and refurbished if needed. The working parts of the engine were cleaned and the boilers were washed to remove mineral buildup daily. Major overhauls occurred about every twelve to eighteen months of service.

Engine houses and roundhouses provided sheltered space for much of this locomotive maintenance. The rectangular engine house required more space for the track to divide and extend to each maintenance bay. The plan, however was better suited to the use of linear cranes, and the proportions of the building were better suited to some sites. Roundhouses required only one track for access with a central turntable that rotated a locomotive so that it was in line with a track that led to a maintenance bay. The diameter of the turntable was determined by the maximum engine length.

There were various other buildings as well, for more specific functions. Toolhouses provided a location to store tools, workbenches, and supplies for maintenance, and replacement parts were fabricated in the machine shops. Breaks in the frame of the locomotive were repaired in the blacksmith's shop. Oil houses stored fuel oils and lubricants. Some railyards had engine-washing platforms. Ash pits were common since a locomotive's firebox needed to be purged of ash and clinkers (irregular lumps of coal left after firing) every four to six hours. Train axles and wheels were removed and reattached in drop pits.

Locomotive Supply Buildings

Some buildings stored and then filled the train with the raw materials locomotives needed to operate: not only coal and water but also sand to prevent wheel slippage in adverse conditions.

Large water towers, usually made of wood, could be found all along the route. Their configuration and size varied, but they were often round, shingled wood tanks supplied with water pumped from nearby sources. Pumping equipment was usually located in a pump house adjacent to the water source. The water tank featured a waterspout to load the water into a train's U-shaped tank, often called a water jacket, located on the tender, the car behind most steam locomotives. In some cases, the water tower had a double waterspout configuration so that two engines could be filled simultaneously.

Coaling towers, also called coaling stations or tipples, stored coal and transferred it to the train. It was first placed in bins, then transferred to buckets that were hoisted to the top of the structure. Loading into the locomotive's coal tender, the empty center of the U-shaped water tank, was through a chute on the other side of the tipple. During the journey, the fireman shoveled coal into the locomotive's firebox as needed.

Sand was heated, dried, and stored in the sand house, to await loading into the dome at the top of the locomotive. The engineer then spread sand on the rails on steep grades or in wet weather.

Freight Car Supply Buildings

Like locomotives, some freight cars had to be filled with supplies before their run. In particular, icehouses were located adjacent to the railroads to load reefer cars with large blocks of ice.

Signage

Railyard buildings were destroyed or sold to avoid taxation, but the railroad's signage, which was not taxed, is often intact. The painted graphics and delicate metal letters of the station identification sign, the trademarks on the railroad cars, and the railroad's safety signage, which reminded workers to "be safe," provide a glimpse into the language, style, and formality of the railroad era.

Buildings for Railroad Workers
Sleeping Accommodations

When the railroad passed through sparsely populated country, the company erected section houses to accommodate the section gangs, comprised of four to six people. When towns lacked even a single hotel, the section house became, on occasion, a makeshift inn, renting extra rooms and providing meals. This occurred in Española when it was a new railroad town on the Denver & Rio Grande's Chile Line. In addition to section houses, the railroad built bunkhouses, houses for the section foreman or stationmaster, and other dormitory buildings.

Like their depots, the Santa Fe Railroad had standards for section houses. The 1910 version was a 24-by 49-foot building with three bedrooms, one bathroom, a kitchen to the rear with a small screened porch, and a back stair to a basement cellar. A screened front porch that extended the full 24-foot width of the front facade led to the living room. The porches, gable roof, and colonial yellow paint are still easily recognizable.

Amenities

At division points, railroads usually provided several amenities for train crews. Railroad hospitals were located in towns such as Albuquerque and Las Vegas, for the thousands of railroad workers that made their homes there.

Reading rooms provided a social center and meeting place for discussion and entertainment as well as a place to bathe and rest at major stops. An article in the *Chautauquan Magazine* in June of 1904 noted that the Santa Fe Railroad "now appropriates some $15,000 a year for maintaining the reading rooms." Each reading room was tended by a librarian, and "after a certain period magazines, weeklies and dailies are sent out from the reading rooms to the trackmen for their homes." The reading rooms were credited to Santa Fe president E. P. Ripley's "belief in more intelligence as a means of securing better service."[2]

Decline of the Railroad

Around the time of World War I, railroad travel in the United States reached its peak. Trackage crested in 1916 at 254,057 miles. Eighty-five thousand stations had been built in the United States. In 1920, the Santa Fe Railroad employed 82,059 people, the most that would ever be on the company payroll, but the railroad built few new depots or depot hotels after the late 1920s. The decline of the railroad has been blamed on the rise of automobiles and airplanes, but the truth is more complex. In other countries these forms of transportation coexist, serving separate functions. The real reasons for such a rapid decline were economic conditions, technological changes and, above all, the federal government's decision to subsidize the automobile and air travel at the expense of railroads.

The Rise of the Automobile

Federal funds, once directed at building track and granting land for railroads, were redirected toward the automobile with the Highway Acts of 1916 and 1921. The result of this legislation was a flood of money that helped states build a million miles of highway between 1919 and 1929. The American obsession with cars and the individual control that they allowed was becoming a phenomenon. In 1900, there were only eight thousand automobiles on the road, but by 1920 there were eight

PART THREE
Preservation

Fig. 13. Abandoned Chile Line grade, 2003. Photo by author.

million. Regular passenger air service began in 1930, offering a speedier alternative to the train for long-distance travel. The "Highways and Horizons" exhibit, also called the "Futurama" exhibit, designed by Norman Bel Geddes for the General Motors pavilion at the 1939 World's Fair, unveiled the automobile-based "City of Tomorrow." Its airports, dense city blocks, open spaces, pedestrian skyways, and motorways were symbols of progress. The exhibit romanticized the notion of the highway, and trains began to be considered outdated and slow.

Economic Conditions

Economic conditions also played a role in the decline of the railroad industry. The collapse of the copper market around 1920 resulted in the closure of company towns such as Tyrone. When the Great Depression devastated the economy only a few years later, people could no longer afford long train trips. Without federal funds,

railroads could not recover from these financial setbacks. Even during the brief revival in train travel during World War II, when trains moved troops across the country, the railroads were dismantling redundant lines in an attempt to consolidate and save funds. The scrap metal of dismantled track was highly valuable to the war effort, and only heavily used lines managed to survive. The loss of trackage was substantial during this period; casualties included the Denver & Rio Grande's famous Chile Line, the Colmor Cutoff, and portions of the New Mexico Central.

Government Subsidies

During World War II, President Franklin D. Roosevelt appointed the National Interregional Highway Committee to investigate the need for a system of national highways for both cars and defense. This system was designed in 1947, and President Eisenhower's Federal Highway Act of 1956 gave government support in the form of road building, subsidies, and tax benefits. The federal government provided 90 percent of the funds, $24.8 billion. In train travel the price of building the track was passed on to consumers in the ticket price; this was not so with road building. If the price of roads were reflected in the cost of automobiles, few Americans could afford cars even today. Government road building accelerated again when, after the war, rubber and gasoline were no longer rationed. The postwar move to the suburbs soon followed, dispersing the population and eliminating trains as a viable commuter option, as they rely on concentrated population centers.

New Technology

Technological advances also changed the way that the railroad operated, leading to more consolidation. The use of oil and then diesel in engines caused railroads to abandon and dismantle lines to coalfields in the late 1930s and early 1940s. In New Mexico, these included the Capitan coal-mining branch and several branches in Colfax County. The widespread use of centralized traffic control in the 1940s, which allowed dispatchers to control switches and signals remotely, and two-way radios reduced the role of the station agent. Small stations, which existed mainly to provide a center of operations in remote areas, eventually closed. In 1967, the U.S. postmaster general announced the termination of almost all contracts with rail carriers. At the same time, even the familiar whistle of an approaching train changed to a mechanized horn; perhaps this symbolized technological progress, but it also symbolized the end of romance in railroads.

In 1970 the government attempted, too late, to save passenger rail travel. The Rail Passenger Service Act passed by Congress in 1970 created the National Railroad and Passenger Corporation (NRPC). Its operating division, Amtrak, purchased cars, formulated a route structure, and began transporting passengers on May 1, 1971. In Europe and Japan rail travel includes government-subsidized high-speed passenger trains, an efficient means of travel with a lower environmental impact that reduces heavy auto traffic. But the United States uses railroads primarily for commercial trade; the few key passenger routes cost far more than budget airlines. The result is a tragic loss of railroad heritage and a move to the suburbs, a dramatic shift in the character of the American town.

CHAPTER ELEVEN

The Current State of New Mexico's Railroads

Currently only seven passenger stops remain in New Mexico. Lordsburg and Deming are along Amtrak's Sunset Limited route from Los Angeles to Orlando. Raton, Las Vegas, Lamy, Albuquerque, and Gallup are along the Southwest Chief route from Los Angeles to Chicago. The stops are basic, with few amenities; Amtrak employees staff the stations just before and after the arrival of the train. Although there were once eighty-five thousand stations in the United States, there are now only about five hundred Amtrak stops, and of these some are just platforms or small prefabricated buildings known colloquially as Amshacks. New Mexico's limited passenger service contrasts with its heavy freight traffic. On average, one hundred trains a day pass by the station at Albuquerque, but only two pick up passengers.

The decline of the U.S. railroad system resulted in consequential casualties. Some railroad buildings—and even entire towns—have been destroyed. Some railroad structures, particularly depots, have been drastically altered. Others have been relocated from their historic contexts.

Among countless structures demolished were the Mission Revival depot in Silver City, the roundhouse in Albuquerque, and the two-story wood-frame depot in San Marcial. But as the railroad destroyed many structures to avoid paying property taxes on its vacant buildings, some depots were saved by their adaptability and movability. However, this adaptability can also be a liability. Depots that were relocated and transformed into restaurants and private homes often lost some historical value, separated from their important trackside or railyard context. Some were extensively altered to serve a new function. Those that are now private homes cannot be enjoyed by the public and are often barely recognizable as depots.

Depots that remain in their original locations were often altered as well. Even as they sat vacant, the railroad companies stripped them of any ornate elements, towers, or second stories to save on maintenance costs and tax assessments. The depot in Deming was once a western-style, two-story building with a shady porch. While still recognizable as a railroad depot, its strange proportions reveal the fact that it has been split, severed, and reassembled. The depot in Roswell, once an excellent example of the application of Eastern Brick style in New Mexico, was stripped of its second story, covered in stucco, and rendered unrecognizable; recently the passenger portion was lost to fire. The missing towers of the Lamy depot, the infilled arches at Clovis, and the spires absent from Raton are more minor changes that can be remedied.

Fortunately, there are also success stories. One of the only narrow-gauge steam railroads remaining in the world, the Cumbres & Toltec Scenic Railroad, operates in New Mexico on a portion of Denver & Rio Grande track from Chama to Antonito, Colorado. The Mexican trestle of the Cloud-Climbing Railroad has been lovingly restored. Depots in Artesia, Las Vegas, and Gallup have received makeovers. The depot at Glorieta still serves as the town's small post office, as it

has since 1964; it looks exactly as it did when the public gathered around to receive mail from the passing
train instead of collecting it inside.

There are still quite a few depots whose fate is yet
to be determined. A renewed interest in preservation of
railroad structures, a better understanding of appropriate uses, and a desire to achieve historically sensitive
remodels will save these significant structures.

CHAPTER TWELVE

Opportunities for Preservation

In 1963, only a handful of architects attempted to stop the demolition of Penn Station, the elegant 1910 Beaux Arts railroad terminal designed by McKim, Mead, and White. While a terrible loss, the destruction of the building eventually caused a public outcry and ignited a preservation movement that eventually led to the 1966 National Historic Preservation Act. The act was created to identify and recognize properties of national, state, and local historic significance and to establish rehabilitation tax credits and other preservation incentives. The ever-expanding official list of historic properties is the National Register of Historic Places, administered and maintained by the U.S. Department of the Interior's National Park Service. Unfortunately, Albuquerque's Alvarado Hotel was not saved by the burgeoning conservation movement, but its 1970 demolition sparked a similar interest in historic structures in New Mexico.

One primary contribution of the preservation movement is the recognition that historic significance can be an economic asset, adding value to a property and increasing visitorship through cultural tourism. The National Park Service has developed criteria for evaluating the historic significance of properties and assessing their historic integrity to determine if they are eligible for the register. But these criteria are helpful even if register status is not desired; they can be used in renovation to assess issues such as the effects of relocation and balancing new functions with historical features in renovations.

Buildings achieve historical significance, according to the National Park Service, through an association with historical events; association with important people; distinctive characteristics of a building type, construction method, or era; high artistic value; or through their potential to yield important information. Most railroad structures are found to be significant because they are examples of a specific building type of the railroad era and are associated with historical events. Significance is established by their place in America's system of railroads, which had a profound impact on this country's culture.

Historic integrity, defined by the National Park Service as "the authenticity of a property's historic identity, evidenced by the survival of physical characteristics that existed during the property's . . . historic period," enables a structure to illustrate its significance.[1] If building features such as setting, materials, and workmanship are intact, it is easier to understand them as products of their time. In renovation projects, the integrity of the structure must be assessed to determine what should be preserved and restored. An original setting that includes other railroad structures, railyards, tracks, and trains is an asset because it provides a context for a railroad structure. Relocation, however, is sometimes necessary.

Assessment of interior and exterior layout, structure, materials, finishes, and features may show structural deficiencies. Other problems include neglect or inadequate maintenance and the results of changes in the intervening years such as missing ornamentation, insensitive additions, new layouts, and new colors. Sometimes historic features such as walls, ceilings, and floors are hidden beneath alterations. The ability of depot buildings to adapt to new functions has caused many changes, but some still contain ticket windows, freight-room scales, train crew graffiti, and telegrapher's desks. Most damage can be restored, missing elements can be replaced, and floor plans and colors can be re-created.

In addition to obvious dangers to railroad buildings—demolition by railroad companies or neglect and subsequent decay—there are also less obvious threats such as the loss of context when a railroad building is relocated, the loss of public use resulting from residential or office conversions, and the effect on travel when a depot is relocated and replaced with an Amshack. Though there has always been interest in railroad buildings, remodelers' intentions often conflict with the preservation of historic integrity. The best use of a depot is as a depot. Where this is not feasible, conversions to transportation hubs maintain some transportation function and public use and require little interior change. If this is likewise not feasible, a depot's historic role as a community gathering place should be honored. Appropriate uses include chambers of commerce, community centers, visitor centers, and museums.

The difficulty of acquiring and renovating railroad buildings creates the possibility that despite a strong advocacy, they may not be restored at all, for any function, even in a new location; they may even be destroyed before these issues can be addressed. Among the obstacles is that railroad companies are wary of allowing buildings to remain where they are. Although old railroad buildings have been fully depreciated and have little value, the land under them can be quite valuable. Railroads may want buildings relocated for safety concerns (many are trackbound between active lines and sidings) or because they fear that an unsuccessful renovation of a building adjacent to their track

will reflect poorly on them. Relocation, however, can be very expensive and even impossible if the building is constructed of anything other than wood.

The cost of restoration can also be an obstacle. Costs include hazardous materials abatement, fencing to address safety concerns, compliance with disabled accessibility requirements and other codes, new mechanical and electrical systems, and general renovation and restoration costs.

As most depots are located in small towns, economics may also be an impediment. Small towns may lack viable potential uses, population, or funds needed to support a renovation project.

There are organizations willing to help with these and other preservation issues. Among them are the New Mexico Historic Preservation Division; the National Trust for Historic Preservation; Amtrak's American Station Fund, which offers technical and design expertise; the State Highway Department's Rail and Intermodal Division; and the Great American Station Foundation, with national headquarters in Las Vegas, New Mexico.

Railroad buildings are beginning to benefit from available resources. Gallup was the first New Mexican depot to be transformed, Artesia's depot now serves as a visitor center and chamber of commerce, and the Las Vegas depot is an intermodal center. Preservation is, above all, dependent on advocacy. It takes only a few dedicated people to revive their local railroad station so that it is once again a neighborhood center and community gathering place.

55

PART FOUR

What Remains of New Mexico's Railroad Heritage

CHAPTER THIRTEEN

Santa Fe Railway System

When Cyrus Kurtz Holliday, the founding father and first mayor of Topeka, Kansas, chartered a railroad in 1859 under the name Atchison & Topeka, he could not have known that it would one day be synonymous with the West. Countless other railroads were being chartered at the same time; most were doomed to fail in the competitive market. Holliday certainly had an idealistic vision. In 1863, before construction of his railroad even began, he changed its name to Atchison, Topeka & Santa Fe Railroad, to add a more exotic destination. Even with a substantial federal land grant, construction did not begin until October 30, 1868; the first seven miles of the road were finally completed in March of 1869. The first locomotive was a 4-4-0 steam engine named after the railroad's founder.

The railroad finally reached New Mexico ten years and a thousand miles later. The mountainous western territories proved difficult for many railroads. One of the only practical routes into New Mexico was Raton Pass, already recognized by travelers on the Santa Fe Trail, who used a twenty-seven-mile toll road operated by Richens Lacy "Uncle Dick" Wootton. Though the Denver & Rio Grande had surveyed the pass, it did not file its location with the Department of the Interior, leaving it open to the first railroad to initiate construction. The Santa Fe (as

Fig. 14. Cyrus K. Holliday locomotive. Courtesy of Great Plains Transportation Museum.

the railroad came to be called around the turn of the century) took advantage of the Rio Grande's oversight.

The legend is that Santa Fe surveyor W. R. "Ray" Morley, a young engineer on his first assignment, was sent to Raton disguised as a sheepherder because the railroad feared that any sign of activity would alert the Rio Grande that it was time to dispatch its crews to take the pass. When two top Santa Fe construction men saw two key Rio Grande engineers headed for Trinidad, sixteen miles north of Raton Pass, they realized that timing was even more crucial. Morley had befriended Wootton; with a promise of $50 a month credit for life at the Santa Fe's store in Trinidad, he put together a makeshift crew of cowboys and local drifters who were sent to the top of the pass in the middle of the night with shovels to begin grading. Only thirty minutes later, the Denver & Rio Grande men found the Santa Fe's crew at work.

As the first to begin construction, the Santa Fe established its right to Raton Pass and became the first railroad line in New Mexico, with track reaching the state on November 1, 1878. On December 7, a 4-4-0 piloted by "Uncle Avery" Turner became the first locomotive in New Mexico. It soon became clear that 4-4-0 locomotives could not negotiate the 3 percent grades of Raton Pass, and a more powerful 2-8-0 was ordered. Named Uncle Dick after Wootton, it was shipped in pieces because much of the existing trackage could not support its fully assembled weight of 115,000 pounds (compared with the 73,000 pounds of earlier locomotives).

After it entered New Mexico, the Santa Fe roared through the territory, building under the subsidiary New Mexico & Southern Pacific Railroad; track reached El Paso, Texas, in June of 1881. The Santa Fe's early lead in New Mexico has proved lucky; the company continues to dominate railroading in the state. The Santa Fe was a financial success partly because it had the foresight to plat numerous towns along the tracks and sell land grant holdings, which created a lasting revenue base. However, it faced an early financial crisis in the late 1880s and again after the Panic of 1893. In 1895 the company was reorganized, and its name was changed from "railroad" to "railway." New president Edward Payson Ripley brought the company out of financial distress the next year by reducing the

Fig. 15. Santa Fe logo from the side of a boxcar next to the Magdalena depot, 2003. Photo by Sharon Wharton.

railroad to a basic network. Santa Fe track in New Mexico was mostly unaffected (with the exception of the Lake Valley mining branch), as it was comprised primarily of key routes. New lines such as the Colmor Cutoff, the logging branches of the Jemez, and the coal branches in Colfax County were purchased or built only after careful study.

By this time the essential features of the company's depots were already established: a gable roof, wooden roof brackets, pedimented door lintels, a hexagonal agent's bay, and double-hung windows with six divisions on the top section and six divisions below. Although many companies standardized some elements of their railroad depots to present a corporate identity and save money, the Santa Fe was the first to standardize floor plans. The "1895 Standards" standardized not only layouts but also paint colors, station sign locations, and quantities of materials. These were revised in 1910, eliminating two-story depots and simplifying details; the "1910 Standards" classify depots as mainline standards or smaller branch-line standards and include standards for section houses and other buildings. Very early depots in other states were barn red, a

color that was later refined to Santa Fe's mineral brown with bronze-green trim and white window sashes. The color was revised again in the 1920s to a colonial yellow, with the same bronze-green trim and white window sashes. There were, of course, special depots for special locations. These were often Mission-style buildings, a style that became linked with the Santa Fe and defined its image.

After the Great Depression, the Santa Fe abandoned more lines in Oklahoma, Texas, and New Mexico. Many mining branches and logging spurs were abandoned, as was the New Mexico Central passenger line to Santa Fe.

Only one new major line was built after 1929. Envisioned as a way to avoid Raton Pass, the Colmor Cutoff was built to connect Oklahoma and Kansas with the Santa Fe's main line at Colmor, a town on the border of Colfax and Mora counties. The line would use seventeen miles of Colorado & Southern track from Clayton to Mt. Dora to avoid track duplication and be constructed by a subsidiary, the Elkhart & Santa Fe Railway. The track reached Farley in 1931; however, with only thirty-five miles remaining to Colmor, work was deferred until economic conditions improved. A weekly train ran to Farley until 1942, when the War Production Board, scouting for seldom-used rail lines to remove for much-needed scrap metal, selected the Colmor Cutoff and the "line that went nowhere" was dismantled for the war effort, along with other western track.

As diesel replaced coal in the 1950s, branch lines to coalfields became inactive, along with the towns on those lines and the depots that served them.

The Santa Fe track that remains is still quite busy with freight traffic. The Belen Cutoff is the preferred freight route linking New Mexico with Texas. The track is now owned by the Burlington Northern Santa Fe, a merger of the Santa Fe and the Burlington Northern, but many of the locomotives on the line are still painted with the familiar blue and yellow (formerly freight) or red and yellow (formerly passenger) warbonnet paint scheme that adorned the Santa Fe locomotives.

The Santa Fe Railway had a lasting effect on railroad travel in the United States. It set the standard for luxurious passenger train service and spearheaded major changes in technology and locomotive design. But the railroad had an even greater effect on the Southwest, linking it with the rest of the country and helping to create its romantic image.

The Santa Fe Main Line: At the Forefront

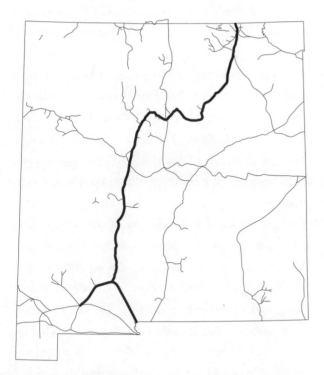

"Ray" Morley, the surveyor of Raton Pass, continued to lay out the best routes through New Mexico for the Santa Fe's main line, which was built by the New

Mexico & Southern Pacific, a subsidiary of the Santa Fe (sold back to the Santa Fe Railway on February 15, 1899). From Raton the railroad's route closely followed the Santa Fe Trail, reaching Las Vegas in July of 1879. It then continued along the Camino Real de Tierra Adentro, the "Royal Road," an early route used by Spanish explorers and colonizers, which earned its name when Don Juan de Oñate cleared the land on behalf of the king of Spain. Tracks reached Albuquerque by April of 1880 and San Marcial in November. At Rincon, the line split, with one branch extending toward Deming and the other toward El Paso. On March 8, 1881 a silver spike joined the Santa Fe with the Southern Pacific Railroad at Deming, creating the country's second transcontinental railroad. Trains arrived in El Paso three months later, creating New Mexico's first interstate railroad. At this point the Santa Fe had 550 miles of track in the territory.

The main line was divided into two divisions. The New Mexico Division extended from the Colorado border to Albuquerque, and the Rio Grande Division ran from there to the Texas border. There were once fourteen stops from Raton to Lamy, eight more to Albuquerque, and thirty-three more to El Paso, with fifty-three depots. Now only fifteen depots from the line survive. Of these, six have been relocated, four are privately owned (including the Abajo depot, which once served lower Albuquerque; the Los Cerrillos depot, now used as a residence in McIntosh; and the Maxwell depot, relocated to Raton and also a private home), and six have been radically altered.

Raton:

Phantom Spires

When the Atchison, Topeka & Santa Fe Railway laid tracks into New Mexico from Colorado in 1879, the

Fig. 16. Passenger depot, Raton, ca. 1905. Courtesy of the Museum of New Mexico, neg. no. 9751.

Fig. 17. Passenger depot, Raton, ca. 1996. Photo by author.

first settlement they encountered was Willow Springs. Notable mainly as a place to obtain water, it was located on the Santa Fe Trail between Uncle Dick Wootton's ranch (which provided supplies for travelers and charged a toll) and the Canadian River, just south of Raton Pass. By 1880 the name of the town had been changed to Raton, an homage to nearby natural features such as Raton Pass and Raton Creek.

The division point at Raton was once a busy railyard with major facilities including a two-story wood-frame depot, a separate freight depot, Harvey House lunch and dining rooms, a company reading room, and a Wells Fargo Express building. The railroad felt the town had such promise that they called it the "Pittsburgh of the West." By 1900, sixty trains passed through Raton each day.

The Raton depot, located west of the tracks at the end of Cook Avenue, was built in 1904 for $30,000. A relatively large depot for Santa Fe's Western lines at around 5,000 square feet, it was a fanciful interpretation of the Mission Revival style that was so commonly used by the railroad for larger cities. The plan was far

more complex than usual, with an octagonal room on the south end that mirrored an octagonal porch on the north. The roof structure was also complex, featuring gables, parapets, and both rectangular and octagonal hips. Tall spires crowned the agent's bay tower and octagonal room; they were tiled and almost Asian in character. The railroad's policy of removing any elements that were difficult to maintain led to the end of the ornate spires in 1920. Other details, such as the tile roofs and quatrefoils above the arched portal, were removed along with the spires. Without them, the depot lacks its former whimsy and graceful proportions. But other distinctive features remain, including the curvilinear parapet walls, elegant arched portal, plaster detailing on the tower, the unusual octagonal southern room, and the two-story tower that extends to the first floor where it becomes the agent's bay.

A Harvey House lunchroom once served hungry passengers traveling through Raton, and a reading room allowed railroad employees to socialize, relax, and expand their minds. The lunchroom, a two-story, red wood-frame building that was next to the original

Fig. 18. Freight depot, Raton, ca. 1996. Photo by author.

depot, opened in 1882 and was closed around 1900, before the current depot was built. Both the Harvey House and reading room are now gone.

However, Raton's freight depot and Wells Fargo Express building remain in their original locations on First Street. The freight depot, constructed in 1903, is located at the end of Galisteo Avenue, south of the depot. It is one of only a few freight depots remaining in New Mexico. The simple structure is constructed of wood frame with board and batten siding and a clapboard base. The yellow paint scheme was typical of Santa Fe depots in the 1920s. Its former use is revealed by the simple gable roof, several freight doors, and freight windows along the south end of the building. The only ornamental feature is the small projecting entry porch with a cross-gable roof.

The Wells Fargo Express building just north of the depot was constructed in the early 1910s. Like the depot, the brick building is covered with pebbledash stucco typical of the time. The small structure echoes the adjacent depot's imaginative interpretation of Mission Revival style. The parapeted ends are scrolled with a vaguely Moorish design, and the windows are arched with small eyebrows. Clues to the building's function include the windows, which were small and high to discourage theft, and a spur extending up to the freight door, which facilitated moving shipped items onto the train. Wells Fargo Express was included in a government consolidation of the major express shipping carriers in 1918; this was bought by an association of railroads in 1929 and became the Railway Express Agency (REA). This is one of only two REA buildings remaining in the state.

The railyard at Raton is still a familiar sight to passengers on Amtrak's Southwest Chief route. Raton is one of only five stops on the route in New Mexico; a portion of the depot still serves passengers.

Las Vegas:
Split in Two by the Railroad

Las Vegas was first settled in 1823 as a stop on the Santa Fe Trail. The town was formally named Nuestra Señora de Dolores de Las Vegas (Our Lady of Sorrows of the Meadows) Although the thriving sheep- and cattle-ranching community was an important stop on the trail, and mail was delivered daily by stagecoach, the town was eager for the train. A railroad representative solicited pledges from local businessmen to bring the railroad through Las Vegas, but it was soon discovered that the rails would bypass the plaza in favor of open land a mile east to avoid additional bridging over the Gallinas River.

The first locomotive arrived on July 4, 1879, and regular freight and passenger service began two days later. The telegraph line, laid in tandem with the track, was put into use only four days after that. Because the next major repair center was Albuquerque, over 130 miles down the line, Las Vegas was designated an important division point. By 1900 it was the largest

Fig. 19. Las Vegas depot, ca. 1900. Courtesy of the Museum of New Mexico, neg. no. 70716.

town in New Mexico and one of the largest wool-shipping centers in the United States. However, the small yet inconvenient distance between the railroad stop and the plaza resulted in the development of what was, in essence, a new town around Railroad Avenue. The area around the plaza, the former heart of the community, became known as West Las Vegas or Old Town, to distinguish it from the rougher, less refined East Las Vegas neighborhood clustered around the tracks. The distinction still remains; Las Vegas is a city that was forever split in two by the arrival of the train.

Las Vegas's first railroad station was a two-story wood-frame depot built in 1881 (which no longer exists). When the important railroad stop warranted a grander replacement, a railroad staff member designed the current depot, which was built in 1898 by Topeka contractor Henry Bennett. The style of the depot is Eastern Brick. In addition to the characteristic hipped dormer window on the trackside, other features of the style include the hipped roof, brick-veneer facade, arched windows, and hipped overhanging eaves that provided shelter to passengers on the platform. As this was a southwestern stop, some Mission

Fig. 20. Trackside view of Las Vegas depot, 2003. Photo by Sharon Wharton.

Revival elements were incorporated, such as a curvilinear parapet at the agent's bay (similar to a remate), with its delicate inset design, and the arched portal on the north end, which serves as an outdoor waiting area.

Despite its fanciful styling, the floor plan and rectangular proportions are typical of most depots. The north-side portal led to the ladies' waiting room. The ticket office and restrooms were located between this waiting room and the gentlemen's waiting room to the south. The ticket office had a view of the tracks from the agent's bay, and the restrooms occupied the corresponding streetside bay. Tickets were purchased in the passage between the two waiting rooms. At the south end of the building were the baggage and freight rooms, which have the telltale small, high windows.

Though the brick base was replaced with concrete

Fig. 22. Trackside view of the Castañeda, 2003. Photo by Sharon Wharton.

Fig. 21. Tower, Hotel Castañeda, Las Vegas, 2001. Photo by author.

sometime between 1900 and 1910, the depot still has its original metal eave brackets, and the original pressed tin ceiling panels have been copied to create replacements. The platform is made of original bricks from Neodesha, Kansas, which read "VVV Brick and T."

Next door to the depot is the well-preserved Hotel Castañeda. The former Harvey House hotel was built at the same time as the depot and by the same contractor for $110,000, with an additional $30,000 of furnishings. Amenities in the 25,000-square-foot building include a lunchroom, a more formal dining room, a large ballroom, and thirty-eight guest rooms, each with their own lavatory and some with a bathtub and toilet. When the hotel opened in 1899, the menu was as opulent as the furnishings, including turtle soup and the famous Harvey House coffee. Ice ponds in the Gallinas River canyon north of Las Vegas were maintained by the Harvey sys-

tem and used to make homemade ice cream.

The Castañeda was the first Mission Revival Harvey House, a style that would become the Santa Fe Railway's trademark. The name, for Pedro de Castañeda de Nagera, the principal historian of Coronado's New Mexican expedition, evoked what was seen as the romantic Spanish colonial era. Architect Frederic Louis Roehrig from California added a deep arched portal around the perimeter of the brick-veneer building, with a shady courtyard and curved parapets facing trackside. He peppered the interior with neoclassical architectural elements and topped the central tower with a baroque crown.

When the Castañeda was the center of Las Vegas society, the now-neglected garden was well manicured, the fountain was a refuge from the desert, and the flowers in the boxes below the second-story windows

Fig. 23. Rawlins Building, Las Vegas, 2003. Photo by Sharon Wharton.

Fig. 24. Roundhouse, Las Vegas, 2003. Photo by Sharon Wharton.

were in full bloom. The hotel hosted the annual Rough Riders reunion from 1899 until it closed. Las Vegas was integrally tied to the Rough Riders, which included twenty local volunteers who served under Theodore Roosevelt when the United States declared war on Spain. Business at the Castañeda was good until the 1930s, and then was revived during World War II when it served as a major troop stop, serving military personnel the same menu at the same dining and table arrangements as it had for years as a luxurious Harvey House. It was not until 1948, after the war, that the Castañeda closed.

Even before the Castañeda opened, the Harvey Company operated a small lunchroom built in 1883 (since demolished). The 1899 Rawlins Building, still remaining across from the Castañeda on Railroad Avenue, served as the mandatory dormitory for the Harvey Girls, the company's able and efficient waitresses. The building is typical of the time, with a flat, parapeted facade and ornately detailed pressed tin siding. Most Harvey Girls considered an assignment at the Castañeda ideal. The job was prestigious, the town was larger than most, and Harvey often accommodated

employees who wanted to take classes at the nearby university. But Harvey Girls had to abide by the company curfew and agree not to marry for the term of a six- or nine-month contract.

The more utilitarian structures of the Las Vegas Division Point were located farther south along Railroad Avenue. The brick-veneer freight depot was the center of wool-shipping operations. The simple building, flat roofed and parapeted with only a small entry portal, was built in 1926 and still remains.

Las Vegas's roundhouse, the semicircular engine-repair shop that survives at the end of the street, was built in 1917 to replace a nine-stall 1880 structure (now gone) when it was deemed inadequate for the major division point. The new thirty-four-stall building cost about $200,000 to build. The principal work in Las Vegas was called "boilerform" and included inspection and repair or replacement of all welded joints, valves, fittings, springs, couplings, and bushings. Although this could not be compared to the complete rebuilding taking place in the engine houses in Albuquerque, twenty or more locomotives were serviced daily in Las Vegas in the 1920s by 380 mechanics on three around-the-clock shifts. The roundhouse was built for function; constructed of brick and concrete with wood doors, it has flattened arches over its windows and a 675-foot inside radius. In 1927, as railroad travel declined, 105 people were laid off from the roundhouse. When diesels were introduced in the 1950s, the turntable that rotated the locomotives toward the bay doors was removed, and the roundhouse was abandoned to the trackside weeds. Although it was never as elegant as the depot and hotel, the roundhouse was a graceful solution to the necessity of locomotive repair; this is one of two surviving roundhouses in New Mexico.

Glorieta:
A New Town at the Top of the Pass

Glorieta Pass at the high point of Apache Canyon is a landmark that has always attracted settlement. The area's trees enhanced the lure of the pass and inspired its name, Spanish for arbor. When the Santa Fe Trail was the prime trading route, a hostelry and stage station known as Pidgeon's Ranch was located at this natural stop.

The location also appealed to the railroad. In 1879, the Santa Fe established a construction camp a few miles west of Pidgeon's Ranch. Its population swelled briefly in 1880 from fifty to two hundred while the budding town was at the end of the tracks. The railroad planned to make it a major stop on its route. But, as was common all over the West, the landowners became greedy, and rather than pay their prices, the railroad put the larger stop at Lamy. The tracks continued to move south, and the settlers followed. After the initial fury of track construction subsided, the population of the area declined and then stabilized. A post office was established on December 17, 1880, named Glorietta for the pass. The name was changed in April 1894 to Glorieta, the correct Spanish spelling.

Fig. 25. Trackside view of Glorieta depot, 2001. Photo by author.

Glorieta's first depot, a two-story wood-frame structure built in 1881, was replaced around 1927 by a small Pueblo Revival–style depot. The construction drawings for the 24- by 61-foot frame and stucco structure are dated June 1926 and signed by Santa Fe Railway staff architect C. A. Harrison. The plan includes a single waiting room at one end, an agent's bay with a telegraph operator's table in the bay, a baggage room, and a freight room with a small closet (called a "warm room" on the plans) adjacent to the agent's area.

The one-sided rectangular bay, Pueblo Revival–style flat roof, and narrow coping are typical of the simplified details of more recent depots. The building displays only a few distinctive Mission Revival elements, including carved wooden brackets, a remate (curvilinear parapet at the agent's bay), and a quatrefoil detail set into the stucco. Very little attention was paid to the facade not facing the tracks; the wall is functional and unarticulated with a small, high freight window, a baggage door at ground level, and a series of windows to provide natural light to the agent's office and waiting room. Unlike earlier structures, the overhang is flat like the roof and the stucco has a troweled finish rather than the traditional pebbledash. A very similar depot, tan with red trim, was built in 1915 in Englewood, Colorado, the only other example of the type. The depot is practical and simple, but with uncomplicated features such as the string course at base level, the battered walls of the projecting agent's bay, and the backdrop of a small wooded hill.

While the layout of the building is unchanged, the depot was converted to a post office in 1964, and the spaces now serve different functions. The waiting room is a foyer, the agent's bay is an office, and the freight room is a mail room. The original ticket window is now used by the postal staff to serve customers. In true New Mexican style, chamisa grows along the tracks and the pace of Glorieta is unhurried; even with its new use, the depot is still the hub of the community.

Albuquerque:
Division Point—Machinists, Blacksmiths, and Boilermakers

On April 10, 1880, the Santa Fe Railway's main line reached Albuquerque; the city, founded by the Spanish, was already 174 years old. In standard fashion, the telegraph line reached the city three days later, and regular train service began two days after that.

Since the tracks had bypassed Albuquerque's historic plaza by a few miles, the railroad platted a new town site with fifty blocks of twenty-four lots each. The Atlantic & Pacific Railroad, in which the Santa Fe owned half interest, platted a 550-lot addition to the south of that. The railroads' economic ventures were successful, and other additions followed. As Vermont newspaper editor Cal Chase noted, "Last February, in the locality of the depot, there was nothing but two or three shanties and a few cloth tents. . . . Today . . . Front St., or Railroad Ave., is solid for

Fig. 26. Alvarado Hotel, Albuquerque, ca. 1910. Courtesy of the Museum of New Mexico, neg. no. 52348.

nearly three quarters of a mile, and lots are selling for as high as $2000." In addition to these commercial lots, home sites were also selling quickly, "for $200 to $500 according to location."[1] The area around the tracks was known as New Town and the plaza began to be referred to as Old Town. One of the first successful businesses was the streetcar connecting Old Town with New Town. It ran down Railroad Avenue (now Central). Other businesses dependent on the railroad, such as foundries, lumberyards, and warehouses, developed close to the track.

Albuquerque was designated by the railroad as a division point, a center of railroad operations and maintenance. It was also the connection point to the Atlantic & Pacific line. Albuquerque's buildings included passenger buildings, freight buildings and, most important, the maintenance and repair shops that kept the railroad and its locomotives in working order.

Passenger Buildings

The public face of Albuquerque's railyard consisted of a depot, a trackside hotel, and its associated museum, shop, and storehouse. The graceful Alvarado Hotel (the largest in the Harvey system), the Indian Curio Building to the south, and the depot south of that were essentially one complex, built in 1902. The interior of the Alvarado was Fred Harvey architect Mary Colter's first project for the company. She was hired to create the interiors for the hotel and the Indian Curio Building, a museum and shop displaying fine American Indian handcrafts. Minnie Harvey Huckel, Fred Harvey's daughter, created the Indian Department to promote American Indian arts and crafts. The success of the Spanish- and American Indian–influenced interiors convinced the Harvey Company to use the style in other hotels and lunch-

Fig. 27. Curio Storage Building, Albuquerque, 2004. Photo by author.

rooms in the Southwest to attract tourists.

The complex of Mission Revival buildings was the heart of downtown Albuquerque. But the Alvarado Hotel and Indian Curio Building closed in 1968 and were demolished by the railroad in 1970. The railroad depot burned on January 4, 1993. All that is left is the trackside wall of the complex and the 1912 Curio Storage Building, later used by the Santa Fe as a traffic office, which has served as a railroad depot since the 1993 fire. The Curio Storage Building is constructed of reinforced concrete, an early example of the construction type. It is typical of simplified Mission Revival style, with a flat roof, minimized ornament (exposed concrete windowsills, string courses, and copings), a stucco finish, and curved parapets. Its small, high windows look almost like those of freight rooms and give away the building's former storage function.

Freight and Operational Buildings

The railyard is also home to freight buildings and operational buildings, including a telegraph office and freight building, which remain in their original locations.

The 1914 telegraph office, once operated by Western Union, is south of the former Curio Storage Building close to the track. It is also of a simplified Mission Revival style, with a flat roof and basic rectangular form. Like the depot and the Alvarado, it is of wood-frame construction with a pebbledash stucco finish, common in the first quarter of the twentieth century. The window shape is typical of railroad buildings, but the elaborate modulated parapet with its wide concrete coping and a concrete string course a few feet from the roofline give the very simple and practical building the appearance of a fancy cake.

Close to the street is the flat-roofed, two-story freight depot. The building has some Mission Revival elements, including curved parapets and a shaded porch that clearly defines the entry. Red neon signage on the street facade reads "Santa Fe Freight House" with "Rail" on one side and "Truck" on the other. The message and the typeface give away its 1946 construction date. The building's details—lintels, sills, base, and canales—are made of concrete, chosen by the railroad for its low maintenance. The gray of the stucco, like that of the Curio Storage Building, is the original color.

Nearer to the locomotive shops is oldest remaining fire station in Albuquerque, built in 1920 (at the time, the Santa Fe provided its own services and utilities). The Rustic Mediterranean–style structure is constructed of random-size sandstone blocks quarried at Laguna Pueblo and taken from a demolished 1881 Atlantic & Pacific roundhouse. Designed by a railroad staff architect, it has a tower, crenelated parapet, and gently arched window lintels. The Atlantic & Pacific division offices were once next to the building, which may explain why its style is so different from the Santa Fe's standard. The only nod to the railroad's typical Mission Revival buildings are the ornamental tile roof

Fig. 28. Freight depot, Albuquerque, 2001. Photo by author.

overhangs and inset Santa Fe cross-shaped logo.

As a major division point, Albuquerque was home to many railroad officials, workers, and staff, so the Santa Fe provided a hospital for its employees and their families. The first railroad hospital in Albuquerque burned in 1903 but was replaced the following year with another structure (now gone). In the mid-twentieth century, the Santa Fe purchased a former tuberculosis sanitarium, consisting of two buildings and a power plant, built in 1926. The complex is now a psychiatric hospital on Central.

Maintenance and Repair

About a half a mile south of the depot and hotel complex are the shops and maintenance facilities—the heart of the Santa Fe's railroad operations in Albuquerque. In 1919, these shops alone employed a quarter of the city's workforce, including machinists, boilermakers, blacksmiths, and welders.

The primary work at the Albuquerque engine houses was the periodic major overhauls of locomotives, which involved stripping them down to the chassis and completely rebuilding them. These overhauls, which took a month to perform, were once necessary every forty thousand miles, but as more durable parts and features were introduced, locomotives could run up to four hundred thousand miles, in service for twelve to eighteen months. The Albuquerque shops serviced about forty locomotives each month; Albuquerque was one of only four facilities, including Cleburne, Texas, and San Bernardino, California, existing for this purpose in the Santa Fe's system.

In 1912, the railroad asked the City of Albuquerque for a $65,000 grant to purchase property to expand and modernize the old Atlantic & Pacific locomotive shops, which were built of wood and stone in 1881 and were

Fig. 29. Machine shop, Albuquerque, 2001. Photo by author.

extremely outdated. With $40,000, the Santa Fe purchased three formerly residential blocks that extended all the way to the Bridge Street overpass. They returned the $25,000 surplus to the city.

The shops were constructed over a ten-year period, beginning in 1914 with the thirty-five-stall roundhouse and turntable, for the daily maintenance and repair of locomotives. The roundhouse was probably the first to follow the Santa Fe's new standardized roundhouse plan; the 1914 standards are dated just before the construction drawings for the Albuquerque version. The standard plan was for a single stall that could be multiplied to produce roundhouses with as many stalls as needed. A taller center section allowed for a clerestory window to provide natural light and a seven-and-a-half ton traveling crane. Though the turntable still exists, the roundhouse has been demolished.

After the roundhouse, a flue shop and storehouse (of reinforced concrete like the roundhouse) were constructed. Around 1917, a steel-frame and brick blacksmith's shop was built, where breaks in locomotive frames were repaired. Smaller buildings included brick locker rooms, washrooms, and a wood-frame sheet-metal shed. These still exist.

The highlight of the Albuquerque shops are the machine and boiler shops, where engines were rebuilt and replacement parts were fabricated. The massive machine shop, 140 by 604 feet, was completed in only eight months, opening in October 1921. It is an example of cutting-edge industrial design from the era, utilizing steel construction, which was increasingly popular for factories because the long spans left more open floor area for configuring assembly lines. The steel frame was composed of a limited set of standardized parts—a few sizes of steel columns and beams, one type of truss, and standard windows; it had spans as wide as 86 feet and was clad with continuous glass curtain walls on the sides. The streetside wall, overlooking Second Street near Pacific, is cast-in-place concrete with large glass openings. The concrete was structurally unnecessary because the steel frame remains behind the facade; the simplified neoclassic styling, with a bracketed cornice below the roof level and a pedimented frieze with the Santa Fe's logo recessed into the concrete, was an attempt to present a less industrial face to the public. With the streetside window configuration, the single-story building (with interior spaces from 30 to 57 feet tall) appeared to be multistory.

The machine shop interior is elegant in its pared-down functionality. The wood floor is made of preservative-soaked wood. Four sets of overhead traveling cranes, which moved the huge locomotives, are integrated into the building's structure. Roof monitors provide even lighting and ventilation throughout the huge space.

A year after the machine shop, the boiler shop was built, employing the same style and construction method, but its concrete facades are obscured by the blacksmith's shop to the east and the fire shed to the west. It is also hemmed in by the flue shop and sheet-metal shed. A sliding transfer table between the machine shop and boiler shop moved the trains from stall to stall; this was a rectangular engine house's equivalent to the roundhouse turntable. The transfer table and its operator's car now sit idly among the weeds; the Santa Fe's safety message, "Safety First: Ship and Travel Santa Fe All the Way," is still painted on the side.

The Albuquerque shops experienced a brief increase in workload when the Las Vegas roundhouse closed after World War II and its boilerform duties were transferred to Albuquerque. However, this consolidation was just the first step in the phasing out of steam locomotives. The Santa Fe began converting to diesel power in the mid-1930s, and after World War II no new steam engines were purchased. In the mid-1950s, the San Bernardino and Cleburne shops were chosen for diesel locomotive repair, and Albuquerque became the central facility for equipment repair and rail line maintenance, requiring only two hundred employees where fifteen hundred were once employed. The last steam engine was retired from the Santa Fe fleet in 1956. The machine and boiler shops are now vacant while interest groups plan their future.

Los Lunas:
The Oldest Depot in New Mexico

The village of Los Lunas was named for the prominent Luna family, headed by Antonio José Luna, "the father of Los Lunas." When the New Mexico & Southern Pacific, a Santa Fe subsidiary, surveyed the area for its line, its preferred route ran through the family's hacienda. Don Antonio José agreed to relocate his family estate, with the stipulation that the railroad would build a new house to his specifications. The Luna mansion was built in 1881 of local adobe bricks, but in an atypical Southern Colonial style with a series of white Doric columns and a bracketed cornice. Don Antonio José died before the house was

Fig. 30. Scissor brackets, Los Lunas depot, 2001. Photo by author.

complete, so his oldest son, Don Tranquilino, occupied the mansion with his family. It was later expanded and is now a restaurant and state landmark.

Before the Luna mansion was complete, the railroad constructed a depot to serve Los Lunas. Completed in 1879, it is the earliest remaining depot in New Mexico. Originally 18 by 88 feet, its freight room was enlarged by 30 feet in 1886 to meet a higher shipping demand. As the station agent needed to observe only the main track, the depot has a single trackside agent's bay; the hexagonal east-facing projection tucks neatly under the gable roof.

The building has undergone many changes over 120 years, including a new 1920s paint scheme of colonial yellow that replaced the original mineral brown (but with the same bronze-green trim, white window sashes, and green roof). Electric lights were finally installed in 1927, despite being common in homes much earlier. As freight traffic decreased, the railroad removed the freight extension, which reduced not only the size of the building but also the property tax. The two coal stoves that warmed the waiting room and agent's office were not replaced with gas heat until 1953.

A year after the depot was retired by the Santa Fe in 1975, the village of Los Lunas purchased it and relocated it from the center of town to its current site. The depot is now painted an inaccurate primary yellow and its windows are boarded up, painted with six divisions on the top half and six divisions below; this pattern does not match the original windows (with four panes over one pane) that still lie beneath the boards. The roof is now asphalt shingles, a low-maintenance and low-cost alternative to the original tin shingles. The freight platform that served the south-end freight room has been removed.

Despite these alterations, the Los Lunas depot still

has many of its original features, which identify it as an early example. The vertical board and batten siding, with its prominent battens, was typical of depots of the era. The gable roof has a deeper overhang (a simple means of providing shelter for waiting passengers) than that used in later depots. These overhangs are supported by a series of scissor brackets, much more complex and finely carved than the triangular brackets that were later used by the Santa Fe. Even the stationmaster's desk, switching levers, and ticket window with its grille and counter are still inside, awaiting a restoration of the oldest depot in New Mexico.

Belen:

Depot and Dining in Hub City

The railyard in Belen is still alive with the smell of diesel and the crashing sounds of train cars coupling. Across First Street there are several flat-roofed, parapeted buildings, vestiges of what was once a very handsome depot district. Some of the details remain: a brick frieze on the side of Pete's Cafe, a faded advertisement on the brick wall of what once was the Central Hotel, and across a small acequia, the Belen depot and Harvey House.

The town of Nuestra Señora de Belen (Our Lady of Bethlehem) has a long history; it was a sleepy farming community on a Spanish land grant from its inception in 1740 until the railroad arrived in 1880. Local merchants were eager for the track to pass through their town and, unlike other communities who held out for better land prices, they contributed to the railroad building to ensure they were on the route. Belen was proud of the railroad, advertising itself as the Hub City and the town "where the trains and trail meet."

Belen was not actually a hub until 1908, when the Santa Fe completed its east-west Belen Cutoff intersecting

the Santa Fe's main north-south line in Belen. A continuation of the cutoff linked Belen and Dalies to create a connection with the Santa Fe's east-west line to California. Within a year, the cutoff was the preferred east-west freight line across the continent. It reduced the distance from California to Chicago by only six miles, but the steepest grade was reduced from 158 feet per mile (at Raton Pass) to 66 feet per mile (at Abo Pass).

In addition to the depot and Harvey House, the railyard once included railroad shops, a coaling station, a roundhouse, and an ice plant, but now only the depot and Harvey House remain. The brick and stucco depot, built in 1909 by Nelson & Sons of Chicago, utilizes simplified Mission Revival details that were characteristic of the railroad's later depots. These include a gabled roof of flat terra-cotta tiles (since removed and sold) and what was once a flat-roofed, open-air waiting room with arched openings that has been enclosed, leaving semicircular windows. The gable roof overhangs the platform on the trackside and is supported with only a few simple wood brackets. In contrast to other heavily carved examples seen on earlier depots, these are two-sided with minimal shaping supporting double beams which, in turn, support roof rafters with scroll-cut ends. The depot also displays Craftsman elements, including the mulled-together windows and cross-gable pitched roof of the agent's bay.

Though the Belen depot has been substantially altered, particularly inside, the adjacent Harvey House (now a museum) is a glimpse into another time. The Harvey House not only provided lunch and dining rooms for Santa Fe passengers and boarding for the Harvey Girl waitresses, it also served as the center of civic affairs in Belen. Residents attended high school dances and ate Sunday meals there, and the Harvey House lawn was one of the only green places in town.

Fig. 31. Belen Harvey House, 2001. Photo by author.

There is some dispute about when the building was constructed, but it was most likely after increased traffic on the Belen Cutoff warranted food service, around 1909 or 1910. The lunch and dining rooms stopped operating within the Harvey system in 1935, but local workers continued service until 1940. The kitchen was reopened during World War II to make box lunches for passing troop trains, but after this brief revival, the railroad converted the building into a reading room where railroad workers could socialize, play cards, and read books and magazines. Some may also have boarded in the former Harvey Girl bedrooms upstairs.

The Belen Harvey House is an excellent example of the Mission Revival style common to New Mexico's Harvey Houses. It has a stepped parapet with a raised coping, flat terra-cotta shingles (which are missing from the adjacent depot), and ornate plaster detailing on the wide chimney. The building's best side faces east toward the tracks. From there, the gable-roofed structure rises up from the flat-roofed, arched portal. The wide platform, made of Coffeyville and Trinidad bricks, continues to the depot, a reminder that this was once one complex.

In 1982, the Harvey House had been vacant and unused for two years, and the railroad planned its demolition. A committee was formed, and the building was saved. The interior was restored, and the Valencia County Historical Society's Harvey House Museum now serves history instead of food.

Socorro:
The Depot on the Wrong Side of the Tracks

As the railroad line extended south along the Rio Grande it encountered well-established towns. Socorro was first settled by the Spanish, who founded a mission in the area in 1598. Don Juan de Oñate named it Socorro, Spanish for "aid," to honor the help (in the form of corn) given to Spanish settlers by the Piro Pueblo Indians. The town was abandoned during the Pueblo Revolt of 1680 and not reoccupied until 1816, when the land was granted by the Spanish Crown to twenty-one families. Socorro expanded when rich mineral deposits were discovered in the nearby Magdalena Mountains in 1867. It grew again with the arrival of the railroad in July 1880, and again

Fig. 32. Freight-door hardware with station agent signatures, Socorro, 1996. Photo by author.

Fig. 33. Crown Mill Company, Socorro, 2003. Photo by author.

in 1885 when a branch was built to Magdalena to ship lead ore from the Kelly mines. Socorro had a smelter to refine the ore, and in the 1890s, it was briefly the largest town in the territory. This distinction was short-lived, however; in 1893 Congress repealed the Sherman Silver Purchase Act of 1890, which had guaranteed government purchase of a certain amount of silver each month. Silver prices dropped sharply, and drought and floods ruined crops. This would have spelled the end of Socorro if not for the opening of the New Mexico School of Mines the same year.

The Socorro depot is a reminder of that boom era. It was constructed in 1888, originally located on the other side of the railroad line. Floods often washed out the tracks during summer storms; one severe flood in 1901 destroyed many of the buildings near the depot and another in 1921 resulted not only in rebuilding of the main line but relocation of the depot to higher ground west of the tracks. During the move, the depot

was not simply rotated so that the single-sided agent's bay faced the tracks. Instead, the bay was removed and reinstalled on the opposite side of the ticket office to avoid turning the structure.

Now located at the end of Manzanares, Socorro's old main street that extends from the plaza, the depot is bound by the main track to the east and a siding to the west. Typical of its time, the depot is made of wood frame with double-hung windows (six panes on the top portion and six below) and a gable roof supported by scissors trusses with scroll-cut ends. The hexagonal agent's bay has a small hipped roof tucked under the gable overhang. This and the lack of a decorative cap on the brick chimney raise the possibility that the depot was once a two-story structure that was converted to one story.

The Socorro depot was originally painted mineral brown, the Santa Fe's standard color for wood-frame depots until the 1920s. It was repainted in 1927 using the new standard, colonial yellow. During an extensive

1959 remodeling, a redwood base and white horizontal asbestos clapboard siding were added, and the trim was painted red, a color combination unique to Socorro. In one location on the east side of the depot, a portion of the redwood base has been pried away, and it is possible to see the original lapped boards of the base, vertical boards of the exterior walls, and evidence of battens, removed to accommodate the new siding. It is an archaeological find, showing vestiges of both mineral brown and colonial yellow paint. During the 1959 remodeling the railroad also lowered ceilings, covered the wood flooring, installed new lighting and plumbing, and replaced the stove with gas heat, but the original ticket window remains.

The last passenger run into Socorro was 1968, but the depot always saw more freight than passenger service. The freight room has its original freight-door hardware and signatures of the men who served as station agents, who customarily signed their names in the freight room upon leaving. To the south along the track are vestiges of the warehouse buildings that once clustered near railroad stops. The Crown Mill Company building, a crumbling adobe with a wood attic, advertises "cement, hard, soft, coal."

San Antonio:
Original Colors

San Antonio is one of many towns in New Mexico named for St. Francis's disciple St. Anthony. Established as a mission in 1629, it was abandoned after the 1680 Pueblo Revolt. In the mid-nineteenth century, the area was resettled, and a post office was established in 1870 by the small community of Spanish farmers. Although the main line of the Santa Fe came through in 1879, the town remained small and isolated until 1882, when an easterly branch line

Fig. 34. San Antonio depot, 2003. Photo by Sharon Wharton.

was built to the nearby coalfields in Carthage.

The San Antonio depot was built the same year, and five years later, Conrad Hilton, founder of the Hilton hotel chain, was born in San Antonio. His father, Augustus Holver Hilton, owned the AH Hilton Mercantile at the corner of Sixth and Main streets, which served the area's miners. When mining traffic diminished around the turn of the century, Hilton converted a portion of the mercantile into a hotel. As children, Conrad and his brother met the trains at midnight, three A.M., and noon to carry passengers' luggage from the station to the hotel.

The depot was 24 by 38 feet, with a two-story passenger portion and a one-story freight room. It was a typical wood-frame depot with a gabled roof, scissors trusses, and board and batten siding. Retired in 1950 and relocated farther down Main Street, it now lies vacant among the weeds, surveying the track it once served. The reddish mineral brown paint that was used extensively by the Santa Fe Railway before

Fig. 35. Original paint where the freight platform has been removed, San Antonio depot, 2001. Photo by author.

Fig. 36. Agent's bay, Hatch depot, ca. 1996. Photo by author.

the 1920s is visible beneath the later coat of colonial yellow paint where the freight platform has been removed. On the sides of the freight room doors, barely visible, is the peeling bronze-green paint, the Santa Fe's standard trim color.

Hatch:
Later Features in a Small-Town Depot

Though the area had been settled in the 1850s, the town of Hatch originated as a railroad stop called Hatch Station in 1881. It was named by the Santa Fe Railway to honor General Edward Hatch, the commander of Fort Thorn, five miles west of the new town. The 1930 depot was one of the last to be built by the Santa Fe, and it served the community of San Marcial until it was moved to Hatch six years later. With the recognition that Hatch was a major shipping point for agricultural products, including local chile, the freight room was extended by 48 feet in 1947. The features that give away the Hatch depot's more recent construction date include a

hipped roof, a minimal overhang without brackets, and a rectangular rather than hexagonal agent's bay. The only brackets used on the structure support the bay's shed roof, a continuation of the main roof plane.

The depot was in service until 1985; when the railroad donated it to the town in 1986, it was moved three blocks south of its original site. The subsequent remodeling transformed the freight room into a library and the passenger portion into a museum, appropriate community uses for what once was a public gathering place. Some original material remains, such as the wood siding—one-by-six lapped boards on the passenger portion and one- by-two on the freight portion. But the rear of the building has been overtaken by humming air conditioning units, large inoperable windows have been installed in the former freight room, and an awkward entry canopy has been added to direct patrons to the library. Although the depot was constructed in 1930 and would have originally been painted the Santa Fe's colonial yellow, the particular yellow and blue used on

Fig. 37. Rincon depot, ca. 1996. Photo by author.

the trim today are not historic colors. The current incarnation of the Hatch depot is an example of how, in the effort to preserve buildings, their historic integrity is often compromised. The interior has some original details but is full of incongruous elements such as the original baggage scale hemmed in by library shelving and the freshly painted, sliding freight-door brackets hanging on white wallboard just below an acoustical tile ceiling.

Rincon:
The Railroad Reconfigures
a Depot to Save Money

The town of Rincon consists of only a few streets and houses and the prominent Mesa Feed Company. The Chihuahuan Desert has claimed back what was once the area's business center. There isn't even a place to eat. Rincon, originally called El Rincon de Fray Diego for a seventeenth-century Franciscan monk who died in the area, took its name from the Spanish word for corner. It is here, just southwest of the depot, that the Santa Fe's main line divides, with one branch extending south to

El Paso and the other going west to Deming. The location along the Rio Grande was chosen for its easy grades, but the river often rose and covered the track. Like the line in Socorro, six miles of track just north of Rincon had to be relocated due to flooding.

Rincon's first depot was constructed in 1881. It was a two-story building with a unique cruciform shape and the agent's bay located at the end so that trains arriving from El Paso or Deming were visible as they came in from the southwest. The current depot replaced the first (now gone) in 1884. It was also a two-story structure, with living quarters on the second floor to house the station agent, a typical configuration in small towns, where it was difficult to find housing. It had a one-story freight addition and a one-sided hexagonal agent's bay. In 1944, the second story was removed, which explains the current arrangement—the flared, hipped roof of the agent's bay tucks under the long gable roof above. If the depot had begun its life as a one-story building, the agent's bay roof would have been incorporated into the main roof structure. The brackets normally seen on depots of this age were eliminated when the roof was

Fig. 38. Las Cruces depot, 2001. Photo by author.

lowered. Though removal of second stories was common, the result at Rincon was an unusual covered platform on the east end, created by the extension of the long gabled roof. It is supported by tall wood posts with western-style post brackets.

Though some original features remain—the freight room door brackets, the board and batten siding, a clapboard base, and double-hung windows—there are few clues to the formerly busy life of Rincon. The Harvey House lunchroom that served passengers from 1883 to 1933 is gone, and all that is left as a reminder that Rincon owes its existence to the railroad are the depot and the tracks to the southeast.

Las Cruces:

The Garden Spot of Southern New Mexico

On the Camino Real, the Royal Road to Mexico City, wooden crosses marked the sites where Spaniards were killed by Apaches defending their territory. At one location, there were so many deaths that it became known as La Placita de Las Cruces (the Place of the Crosses). A town was officially established there in 1848, and in 1852 Las Cruces became the county seat of Doña Ana County. By the 1880s, with the Apaches defeated, Las Cruces was a quiet Hispanic farming community; nearby La Mesilla was the larger center of trade and commerce. This would soon change when the Santa Fe Railway bypassed La Mesilla and instead built the tracks through Las Cruces, opening markets for the local agricultural products and transforming the tiny town into an economic and transportation hub.

A group of entrepreneurs, seeking to make a profit from the railroad, bought farms west of town and sold some of the land to the railroad for their right-of-way. The remainder, between the railroad tracks and the original Las Cruces town site, they divided into residential lots. This became Las Cruces's first suburb, a forty-two-block area with the depot at its heart, settled by wealthy Anglos. They built elaborate homes in an assortment of styles including Mediterranean villas, Colonial Revival mansions, Prairie Style bungalows, Neo-Classic Revival estates, and Italianate Victorians. Most borrowed regional adobe elements from homes in the adjacent cohesive

Hispanic neighborhoods. Fourteen architectural styles are represented in what is known as the Alameda-Depot Historic District, and four homes were designed by prominent El Paso architects Trost and Trost. The residents utilized the old acequias, irrigation ditches that once provided water to the farms, to irrigate their lawns and ornamental gardens. In sharp contrast to the dusty streets of the original townsite of Las Cruces, the city began to be known as the "garden spot of southern New Mexico."

The railroad depot, located appropriately on Depot Street, now Las Cruces Avenue, had its own wide lawn. The building was built around 1910 by Albuquerque contractor A. W. Anson to replace an 1881 wood-frame depot that was hauled by flatcar to La Tuna (later Anthony), New Mexico. The standard depot was no longer grand enough for the developing city. The new depot followed the Santa Fe's brick "county-seat" depot plan used extensively on its western lines. In locations like Norman, Oklahoma; Harper, Kansas; and Fowler, Colorado, the brick was left exposed, but the New Mexico depots were coated with pebbledash stucco and roofed with red tile—Mission Revival features that the Santa Fe used in the Southwest. The open-air waiting room common to county-seat depots was eliminated at Las Cruces in favor of a long, low freight room that was extended in 1961.

The county-seat depot characteristics include a symmetrical gable-roofed passenger portion with parapeted ends and waiting rooms on either side of the agent's bay. The parapets are pitched like the gable, in contrast to true Mission Revival parapets with their undulations. At the peak is the Santa Fe's logo: a cross inscribed in a circle incorporated into the concrete coping. The overhanging roofs are supported by brackets, typical of depots, but the end brackets rest on pilasters that project from the facade. The trackside agent's bay, with a semicircular window, is mirrored on the street-side with the public door. The freight/baggage portion has a flat roof with an articulated, stepped parapet.

The depot had many of its historic features intact when it was restored in the late 1990s. Double-hung wood windows (with six divisions on the top sash and a single pane below), chair rails, cabinetry, and an ornate ticket window with diamond-shaped leaded glass and an ornate metal grille were retained, and the passenger platform is still paved in Coffeyville bricks, a testament to their durability.

Mesilla Park:
The Deco Depot

Mesilla, an important stop on the Butterfield Overland stagecoach, was named for its location on a small mesa above the Rio Grande floodplain. The busy town lost its county-seat status to nearby Las Cruces in 1852. Soon after, a company was formed to sell off farmland east of the village. The result was a new townsite called Mesilla Park, which flourished when the Santa Fe Railroad routed its main line to El Paso through the area in 1881. When the state agricultural college, now New Mexico State University, was built nearby in 1889, Mesilla Park's future was secured. Las Cruces has since absorbed both La Mesilla and Mesilla Park.

In 1925 a new brick and stucco depot was constructed to replace an earlier frame structure. Located southwest of the interstate, the Pueblo Revival building has typical southwestern features such as stepped parapets, buttresses, recessed windows, and flat roof. The agent's bay parapet is a departure from the overall symmetry of the building, stepping higher to the south. Art deco details reveal its construction date; the top pane of the narrow windows has a deco leaded design—three

Fig. 39. Mesilla Park depot, 2001. Photo by author.

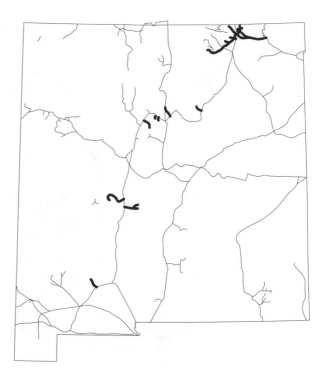

vertical bands with a diamond inscribed in the center—and deco letters spell the station name.

The Mesilla depot has a typical railroad station layout. The building's long axis runs parallel to the Santa Fe's main line. The agent's bay, a solid-looking projection on the west facade, faces the tracks. And the freight room on the south is unmistakable, with a baggage door at ground level and two freight doors at railcar level.

The low concrete base was once painted a darker, contrasting color, and the window trim was once green. Though the building is tattered and has been altered by the railroad, it awaits a revival of its former Pueblo Deco elegance.

Santa Fe Branch Lines: Mining and Tourists

In addition to the Santa Fe's main line, which raced across the state to connect with other railroads, the Santa Fe also built several branches. Some were constructed to reach important cities such as Santa Fe, others led to gold and silver mines, and at least one ferried tourists to a luxurious getaway. Many accessed the Santa Fe Railway's coalfields to provide the fuel necessary for steam locomotives.

Santa Fe Branch

The Santa Fe's main line was not built through the railroad's namesake; the official reason was the difficult grades of mountain ranges. There was much speculation about other potential reasons, including an anticipated decline in trade in Santa Fe coupled with a rise in agricultural trade in the Rio Grande valley and the need to please the members of the territorial legislature, most of whom lived along the main route. Santa Fe subsidiary New Mexico & Southern Pacific built a branch line instead; it split from the main line at Galisteo Junction, later renamed Lamy, and reached the territorial capital on February 9, 1880. The Santa Fe Railway owned the branch until 1992. The Santa Fe Southern now operates an excursion train on the line.

Fig. 40. Santa Fe Southern engine, ca. 2001. Photo by Sharon Wharton.

Fig. 41. Santa Fe depot, ca. 2001. Photo by Sharon Wharton.

Lake Valley Branch

The branch line to Lake Valley was built by the New Mexican Railroad, another Santa Fe subsidiary, from Nutt, a main-line station between Deming and Hatch. The branch served the mining area from 1884 until it was dismantled in 1893. The railroad facilities at Nutt were destroyed, but the tiny Lake Valley depot remains, seriously threatened by neglect.

Hot Springs Branch

The 6.4-mile branch from Las Vegas west to the Santa Fe's resort at Hot Springs was constructed by the Santa Fe's subsidiary New Mexico Railroad Company in 1882. A depot once received the guests of the Montezuma Hotel as they departed the train. It was demolished and the original hotel burned in 1884, but the grander structure built to replace it in the late 1880s looms castle-like over the small valley.

Magdalena Branch

The Santa Fe's Magdalena Branch was built in 1885 by Santa Fe subsidiary New Mexican Railroad to serve the mines west of Socorro. A two-mile branch was extended to Kelly, center of the mining district, that same year, with ore sent to Socorro smelters. Soon after the twenty-six-mile line was put into service, Magdalena became a livestock shipping center. Though the small branch remained active for years, the traffic slowly faded, and the line was dismantled in 1972.

Coal Branches

One of the primary needs of locomotives in the late nineteenth and early twentieth centuries was coal to turn water into steam for power. Many Santa Fe branches were built to access New Mexican coalfields.

When the Santa Fe built its main line south, it also built a ten-mile branch from San Antonio to the coalfields

Fig. 42. Santa Fe depot station sign reflected in railcar window, ca. 2001. Photo by Sharon Wharton.

at Carthage. The line, under the name New Mexican Railroad, was completed in 1882 and operated until about 1895. It was dismantled in 1896 because of a rumor that the coal was exhausted. When this proved untrue, coal had to be shipped by wagon to San Antonio. In 1906 the line was rebuilt on the Santa Fe's old grade by the mine's owner, Carthage Fuel Company, using a subsidiary company called the New Mexico Midland Railway. Another branch was built to the north to access the Hilton Mine, owned by Conrad Hilton's father. The mines truly were depleted in 1925, train traffic ceased in 1931, and the lines were once again abandoned in 1933.

The mines in Cerrillos and Madrid are some of the oldest coal mines in the West, dating from 1835. In 1892 the Cerrillos Coal Railroad Company built a line from the main-line stop at Waldo south to Madrid, six and a half miles away. The Santa Fe purchased the railroad under foreclosure in 1901. Mining production did not cease until 1954, and the railroad was abandoned in 1960.

By 1905, the Santa Fe had sold most of its coal mines in response to public criticism over railroad monopolies and because mining subsidiaries yielded such low profits.

But steam locomotives still had their insatiable appetite for coal. Several companies began mining operations in the early 1900s in coal-rich Colfax County. They often built their own railroads to access these fields, but realizing that it was costly to operate both mines and railroads, they sold their lines to their primary customer, the Santa Fe, and concentrated on mining coal.

One example was the St. Louis, Rocky Mountain & Pacific Railway, formed by Hugo and Harry Koehler of St. Louis, Jan van Houten of Raton Coal and Coke, and Charles and Frank Springer, who owned portions of the Maxwell Land Grant. The system was called the Swastika Route, after the Swastika Fuel Company, named for the ancient American Indian symbol. Its lines, built around 1906 and 1907, snaked through the hilly region to mines and railroad stops, often named for the system's founders. Springer is off of the Santa Fe's main line, but Van Houten and Koehler are on spurs off the line to Cimarron. They sold their track to the Santa Fe Railway in 1913, which operated the lines under the name Rocky Mountain & Santa Fe Railway beginning in 1915. There were once five depots on what the Santa Fe referred to as its Rocky Mountain Branch, but none survive; most of the lines have been dismantled.

In 1924, the Santa Fe purchased another coal company's railroads. The Sugarite Branch was built by the Santa Fe, Raton & Eastern, a subsidiary of the Yankee Fuel Company between 1906 and 1908, but had been bought by the New Mexico Coal Company in 1911. Though the lines served Yankee, Carrisbrook, Lake Alice, and Sugarite, the line was devoted to coal, and there were never any depots.

Santa Fe: Welcoming Tourism
Whether the reason was difficult grades, a lower volume of anticipated traffic, or political maneuvering, the

Santa Fe's main line did not pass through Santa Fe, the territorial capital that gave the railroad its romantic name. The residents of the city were dismayed. Even before New Mexico was a territory of the United States, Santa Fe was the Spanish colonial capital of the region. There may have been settlers there even before 1610, when governor Don Pedro de Peralta was instructed by the viceroy to establish the town for the "Kingdom of New Mexico." Peralta named the community La Villa Real de Santa Fe to honor the original Santa Fe, outside Granada in Spain. At the terminus of both the Santa Fe Trail and Camino Real trade routes, the most important town in the region was accessed only by an eighteen-mile spur from the main line at Galisteo Junction, later renamed Lamy.

Governor Lew Wallace, author of *Ben Hur*, drove in the last spike in February 1880 to complete the connection, symbolically drawing the era of the Santa Fe Trail to a close. Santa Fe residents immediately contracted a case of railroad fever: the new Broad Gauge and Narrow Gauge saloons and Santa Fe's first depot were built the same year (all are now gone). The unassuming frame structure was converted to freight use and replaced with something more impressive in 1909 in response to the handsome brick depot built by the company's rival the Santa Fe Central. At this time the station received a modest four trains a week.

The masonry depot was constructed of brick and coated with brown pebbledash stucco. Its layout consisted of four rooms: separate men's and women's waiting rooms, an agent's office with a bay window facing the tracks to the northwest, and a baggage room on the northeast end. On the southwest, a portal with rectangular stepped openings and a flat roof creates an exterior covered waiting room. On the streetside, the slight overhang of the red-tile roof is supported by curved wooden brackets with scroll-cut ends, a very different bracket from the scissors-type found on frame depots. On the trackside, the agent's bay facade incorporates a semicircular and stepped parapet, an element borrowed from the California missions. The Santa Fe depot is nearly the twin of the Lamy depot, built the same year.

After passenger service on the line was discontinued and the depot was closed in the late 1920s, the Clarkson Bus Company transported passengers from the junction at Lamy to Santa Fe's La Fonda Hotel, which also sold railroad tickets. La Fonda, built by Rapp, Rapp, and Hendrickson in 1920, was purchased by the Santa Fe Railway in 1926. The renovation of the reinforced concrete structure began immediately, under the direction of Harvey Company staff designer Mary Colter. Colter, working with prominent architect John Gaw Meem, expanded the hotel from 46 to 156 rooms with an addition and a new fifth floor. Tinsmiths created custom light fixtures, and local artists such as Olive Rush were commissioned to paint murals and glass to complement the hotel's vigas, towers, terraces, balconies, and battered stucco walls.

La Fonda was the headquarters for the Harvey Company's Indian Detours. Train passengers could purchase tickets that included stopovers at the Grand Canyon, Albuquerque, Santa Fe, or Gallup as well as one-, two-, and three-day trips with guides. In 1931 the Harvey Company sold the operation to Clarkson, which cancelled all but the tours out of Santa Fe; these, too, were terminated around World War II. Train tickets for trips leaving from Lamy station were still sold at La Fonda until 1968.

Still remaining as tributes to the railroad's importance in the capital are the La Fonda (sold in 1969), the small masonry depot, and warehouse buildings along Guadalupe Street that owed their livelihood to the railroad.

An excursion train, the Santa Fe Southern, now runs on the Santa Fe's spur. It borrows its name from a dream that was never realized. In 1889, the Texas, Santa Fe & Northern, which operated a line from Santa Fe to Española that connected to the Denver & Rio Grande's line to Colorado, incorporated the Santa Fe Southern Railway. The goal was to build from Santa Fe to the mining camps of Cerrillos and further south. The railroad's financial troubles delayed the project indefinitely, but its name is honored by the new Santa Fe Southern.

Lamy:
On the Road to Santa Fe

When it was determined in 1880 that the territorial capital would be located on a branch line rather than the Santa Fe's main line, the railroad established a connection point for the branch called Galisteo Junction, a site known to Spanish settlers, who grazed sheep there. The budding town was located in the center of the Lamy land grant, taken in trust for the church by the diocese's first bishop, Jean Baptiste Lamy; its name was changed to Lamy in his honor in 1881.

Those who took advantage of the initial lawlessness of new railroad towns—gamblers, criminals, and the so-called bunko steerers, con men who swindled people in card games—were drawn to Lamy. The Santa Fe sheriff came regularly to make arrests, and by 1889 Lamy was a respectable community.

Lamy's first depot was built in 1881, a two-story wood-frame structure that was converted for freight use when a new brick depot was built in 1909. Like the depot and Hotel Castañeda in Las Vegas, the new Lamy depot was constructed by Topeka contractor Henry Bennett. Its simplified Mission Revival style was typified

Fig. 43. Lamy depot, ca. 1996. Photo by author.

by a stucco finish, gabled roof of red tile, and an east-end open-air waiting room with wide arches. Originally this open breezeway had a flat, parapeted roof with stepped corners, but a gable roof was added. The rectangular agent's bay, overlooking the tracks to the south, was once the lower portion of a square tower with a hipped tile roof. The tower was removed in 1933; left without a wall surface for a sign to identify the station on the trackside facade, the railroad perched metal letters spelling "Lamy" on top of the agent's bay. In 1941, a freight room with a gabled roof like the breezeway was added to the simple structure, and the freight depot (the first passenger depot) was retired. It is now gone.

To the east of the depot, now a grove of trees, was the El Ortiz, a Harvey House designed by Kansas City architect Louis Curtiss with interiors by Harvey Company staff designer Mary Colter. The grand hotel was a one-story Pueblo Revival oasis with around ten guest rooms grouped around a patio. William Jennings Bryan and William "Buffalo Bill" Cody were guests, among other notables. The hotel operated from 1910 to 1938. The junction at Lamy also once had a roundhouse and an extra "helper" locomotive that was added to northbound trains on the main line

Fig. 44. Lamy depot breezeway, ca. 1996. Photo by author.

Fig. 45. Agent's bay, Magdalena, 2003. Photo by author.

to push them over 8,000-foot Glorieta Pass.

In 1926, the Santa Fe Railway ceased operations on the eighteen-mile branch to Santa Fe. A "Harvey Car" began bringing passengers, mail, and baggage to the capital city. El Ortiz was demolished in 1943, and the switch from coal to diesel in the 1940s eliminated the need for the roundhouse and helper engine. But, with its platform of Coffeyville bricks, an old Railway Express Agency cart to move baggage, and the original freight-room scale, the Lamy station still serves as the main-line stop for rail travelers to and from Santa Fe.

Magdalena:
Where the Hoof Highway Meets Hard Scramble

Magdalena began as a mining community in 1866 when rich lead deposits were found by J. S. "Old Hutch" Hutchason. Regarded as the father of the Magdalena mining district, he staked the Juanita, Graphic, and Kelly mines. The ore was smelted locally in adobe furnaces and an ox team hauled the metal to Kansas City. Hutchason sold his mines in the late 1870s, and in 1881 he erected a smelter near Socorro

to treat the ore from area mines, including the Iron Mask and Hard Scramble.

The Santa Fe Railway sought to profit from the region's lead-mining boom and in 1885 built a twenty-seven-mile spur from Socorro to Magdalena to haul ore. The line climbed 2,000 feet in only sixteen miles and was therefore dubbed the Elevator. Since the grade to the mining camp at Kelly was initially considered too steep for a spur, a daily stage, pulled by sixteen-mule and -horse teams, operated from Kelly to Magdalena.

With the completion of the Socorro Branch, stockmen from Arizona and New Mexico began driving livestock east over the Plains of San Agustin to the train at Magdalena for shipping. This was the beginning of the Magdalena Stock Driveway, informally known as the Beefsteak Trail or Hoof Highway. The village became one of the largest livestock-shipping points west of Chicago (21,677 head of cattle and 150,000 sheep transferred to the train in 1919). There was often animosity between the miners and ranchers, but the con-

Fig. 46. Waiting room end, Magdalena, 2003. Photo by Sharon Wharton.

current shipping of livestock and ore continued. When Magdalena became the smelting town for Kelly in 1896, the *Las Vegas Optic* reported: "The town is very orderly at present, but generally keeps up its reputation as a frontier town at the terminus of a railroad."[2]

As the lead deposits diminished in the 1890s, miner Cory T. Brown of Socorro tested the green rock that was discarded during mining operations and found it to be smithsonite, a zinc carbonate valuable for its use in paint production. Brown and other mine owners sold their claims to paint companies such as Sherwin-Williams and revived mining in the region until 1931, when these deposits were exhausted as well. The cattle trail continued until the railroad terminated the Magdalena Branch in 1971.

The clearinghouse for livestock and ore was Magdalena's railroad depot. The first depot, built in 1885 (which may still exist as a private residence), was replaced in 1915 by a "No. 4 Standard for Branch Lines" with an extended freight room to handle shipping demands. The layout included an agent's office with small hexagonal bay window typical of branch lines.

There was a waiting room on either side of the agent's office, each with a ticket window; the room on the west end served women and the other served men. Off the men's waiting room was a baggage room; beyond that was the freight room. The standard bill of materials for the "No. 4" lists every item needed to build the depot, including lumber, doors, windows, hardware, and paint. The paint colors included Sherwin-Williams no. 2551 (Santa Fe's mineral brown) for the exterior, paint no. 2616 (bronze-green) for exterior trim, maple green or bright sage for the interior walls, and buff stone, no. 839, for the interior ceiling. Even the stain for the interior trim and wainscot was specified.

Though the colors were changed to Santa Fe's new standard colonial yellow in the 1920s, the depot has been returned to its original color scheme. Inside, the ticket window, narrow board ceiling, wainscot, vertical siding, and five-panel doors are intact. Though the freight room is now used as a library, the signatures of past station agents—Right Hook Hill, Joe McCarty's, and WC, among others—still adorn the walls. The depot, retired in 1961, remains an important public building; in addition to the freight-room library, the agent's office and waiting rooms are used for the village hall.

Across the street is a red brick, gable-roofed warehouse remaining from a time when warehouses claimed advantageous trackside positions. It was built in 1913, with an unusual roof monitor that fills its interior with natural light. It was purchased by the Charles Ilfed Company, one of the largest mercantile companies in New Mexico. Known as "Wholesalers of Everything," the company was founded in Las Vegas in the 1870s. Western ranchers relied on such establishments, buying supplies against future receipts from the sale of cattle and sheep.

Magdalena is named for a rock and shrub forma-

Fig. 47. Charles Ilfeld Building, 2003. Photo by author.

Fig. 48. Passenger depot, Lake Valley, ca. 1996. Photo by author.

tion said to resemble the profile of Mary Magdalene on nearby Magdalena Peak. The face is less distinct since the drought of 1950 to 1952 killed many of the shrubs that shaped the face on the east slope, but Mary Magdalene still watches over the town. Although its population hovers around a thousand, there is still both ranching and mining in the area, and the community is vibrant and independent, with a rich history and strong reminders of its railroad past.

Lake Valley:
Silver Boom and Bust

Although silver was first found in the Lake Valley area in 1878, the town owes its existence to the 1882 discovery of the Bridal Chamber, one of the richest single-ore bodies ever discovered. Found by blacksmith-turned-prospector John Leavitt, it produced 2.5 million ounces of silver. The ore was so pure it was sawed and cut into blocks instead of being blasted. Leavitt made his strike only a few yards away from the Columbia Mine, purchased the previous spring by George Daly, owner of Sierra Grande Mining Company for $225,000. The Columbia Mine was sold by George W. Lufkin, an ex-railroad engineer from Maine, and his

partner, Chris Watson. Lufkin reinvested the money in real estate, establishing a town site nearby and selling lots; he named the town Daly for the man who bought his claim. Leavitt sold his Bridal Chamber claim to the Sierra Grande as well. Owner George Daly was killed by Apaches, six miles west of town on the day of Leavitt's discovery of the huge silver deposit.

Daly, Lufkin's town, was moved slightly and renamed Sierra Grande, for the mining syndicate. It moved again in 1882 and was renamed Lake Valley—ironically, since the town's main problem was a lack of water. It may have been named for a shallow pond north of town that was created during the summer rainy season and was the only body of water for miles around. Lufkin continued to move with the town, and spent the rest of his life there.

Although Lake Valley was booming, with a population of a thousand and no vacant hotel rooms, the ore was still shipped by stage between Lake Valley and the Santa Fe Railway station at Nutt, about fifteen miles south on the main line to Deming. The fare was $2. Expecting a lot of freight, the Santa Fe finally completed a spur to the rich mining district in 1884. The train brought the mail and took back ore

Fig. 49. Railroad grade with Lake Valley passenger depot, ca. 1996. Photo by author.

to be refined elsewhere. Lake Valley was the shipping point for the entire area: gold and silver were transported on stagecoaches that came from the nearby towns of Hillsboro and Kingston.

Lake Valley grew into a proper town, with Main Street intersecting Railroad Avenue, and a railroad depot was built in 1885. It was separated into two small buildings, an alternative to the combination passenger and freight depot. The passenger depot also served as the town telegraph station.

Lake Valley, despite early promises of prosperity, was plagued with bad luck. When Congress repealed the Sherman Silver Purchase Act in 1893, it caused the devaluation of silver; this affected many New Mexican mining towns, including Socorro, but devastated Lake Valley, which relied only on its silver. Mining operations ceased that year, and only two years later, most of the buildings on Main Street, so closely spaced together, were destroyed by fire.

The train, however, ran daily for fifty years. The abandoned branch was removed in 1934 and was not replaced despite the discovery of manganese ore and a subsequent brief mining revival from 1934 to 1943. The depot was purchased from the railroad by Lake Valley

resident Blanche Wilson Nowlin as a memento after the 1937 death of her husband, Slim, who had been Lake Valley's railroad superintendent. She protected it from vandals until her death in Lake Valley, by then a ghost town, in 1982. The depot is the only Santa Fe structure with its original mineral brown paint and bronze-green trim, though they are badly faded. The structure is now crumbling, but the board and batten siding, double-hung windows, remnants of the interior wood wainscot, cabinetwork, and even a white ceramic doorknob remain. The freight depot has already collapsed.

Most of Main Street is just foundations since the fire, but there is an old stone building at the intersection of Main and Railroad, which served over the years as a school, saloon, general store, and gas station. The railroad coal sorter is still on the end of Railroad Avenue. An old mineshaft below the sorter yielded a small amount of water to supply the train. From the coal sorter you can see the notch in the hillside where trains emerged, passed the sorter, and edged to the right of the water towers and on to the depot and mines.

Montezuma: The Phoenix

To increase its revenues, the Santa Fe Railway often developed related ventures, particularly tourist attractions. In the late 1870s, the railroad purchased the Las Vegas Hot Springs Company, including eight hundred acres and hot mineral pools west of Las Vegas. Santa Fe Railway officials were placed on the board of directors and work began on a hotel and health resort to attract tourists and "health seekers" who sought the therapeutic springs and the dry, clear climate of northern New Mexico. The hotel, completed in 1879, was modest, but featured lodging and dining managed by the Fred Harvey Company, so the quality was superior.

In February 1882, while a grander hotel was under

Fig. 50. Montezuma Hotel, ca. 2002. Photo by author.

Fig. 51. Montezuma power station, ca. 2002. Photo by author.

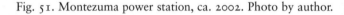

construction, grading began on the Santa Fe's six-mile Hot Springs Branch to Montezuma. The first trains arrived on April 9, and the hotel opened eight days later. The opulent structure designed by Jerome, Rice, Moore, and Emery of Kansas City cost $200,000 and took fifteen months to built. There were 270 rooms furnished in a Queen Anne style, a dining room with eight chandeliers, four billiard tables, four bowling alleys, archery, and lawn tennis. Five special trains left Las Vegas each day, at 8:05, 10:20, 12:30, 5:45 in the evening, and 7:55 at night. The trip took forty-five minutes and the train allowed for stopover privileges, though the wealthy often preferred driving in private carriages. All were greeted with music and bellhops in blue and brass.

The first hotel burned in 1884 but was replaced by an even more imposing structure designed by Chicago architects Burnham and Root. The new four-story

stone hotel, called the Phoenix, had 250 rooms and was built for $300,000. Despite the incorporation of the latest fire-prevention methods, when a blaze started in the attic the year after it was built, the hotel was damaged beyond repair.

Undaunted, the Santa Fe Railway built another hotel in Hot Springs, now called Montezuma, around 1886 for $800,000. Often referred to as Montezuma Castle, the Queen Anne Victorian still surveys the valley from its mountainside location. The three-story stone and shingle structure has several turrets, including a large round tower with a conical shingled roof and wraparound widow's walk. A dramatically tall gable roof and both open and enclosed porches once provided a variety of places to enjoy the view. Inside there are finely crafted stairs, carved ash ceilings, and a welcoming entry fireplace.

The Santa Fe closed the Montezuma on October 31, 1903, after it determined that a resort at the increasingly popular Grand Canyon would be more profitable (El Tovar on the canyon's south rim opened in 1905). The railroad sold the Montezuma's magnificent furniture to the St. Louis World Fair Hotel and demolished the depot. Floods soon swept away the bathhouse, but the power station, a stone building with a tall brick tower, remains. The Las Vegas & Hot Springs Electric Railway continued to serve Montezuma until 1937, when the line was dismantled. The hotel is now used by the Armand Hammer United World College (which provides guided tours).

The Belen Cutoff: When Longer Is Shorter

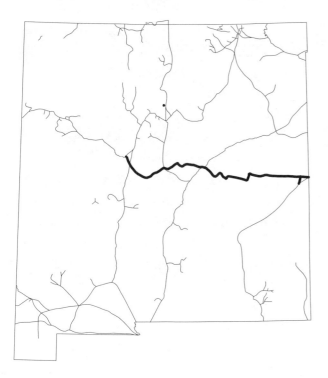

With a working line traversing New Mexico, the Santa Fe dominated railroading in the state. The route, however, required negotiating the 3 percent grades at Raton Pass. Although engineer Lewis Kingman had an idea for a cutoff even while the Santa Fe was building its main line, no one investigated the area until the turn of the twentieth century. By this time, traffic on the line caused bottlenecks at the pass that affected operations in the rest of the system. Grades were also difficult at the mountain pass at Glorieta, and a direct connection between the Santa Fe's Texas and Coast lines was needed for interstate shipping.

Using a tactic that was employed repeatedly, the Santa Fe acquired an existing railroad that was in financial distress to augment its own system. The Pecos Valley Railroad extended from the panhandle of Texas north into New Mexico. With a large gap between this line and the Santa Fe's main line, in 1901 the railroad dispatched its surveyors into the plains of eastern New Mexico to plan a route that would link Belen with Amarillo, continuing to the Santa Fe main-line station of Newton, Kansas. The junction with the Pecos Valley Railroad would occur in Texico.

On October 30, 1902, the Santa Fe created a subsidiary, the Eastern Railway of New Mexico, specifically to build the line, and grading began in 1903. Since Abo Pass, at the Continental Divide, was the steepest and therefore most complex portion to build, construction began there early in the year. But by July, only twenty miles had been graded, and the Santa Fe shelved the project for financial reasons. Work resumed in 1904, when a small segment was built from the Rio Grande to Belen at the westernmost part of the cutoff. The following year, work began at the eastern end of the line, from Texico to Fort Sumner/Sunnyside. The line continued to be built from both ends working toward the middle until it was completed in 1908. The same year, the Santa Fe shifted the connection with the Pecos Valley Railroad from Texico to Clovis when they built a short spur to Clovis from Cameo.

The Belen Cutoff is actually longer in distance than

Fig. 52. Former freight depot sign, ca. 2000. Photo by author.

Fig. 53. Clovis depot, ca. 1996. Photo by author.

the route through Raton Pass and has the longest continuous grade in the Santa Fe system, a 148-mile section from Fort Sumner to Mountainair, but the ruling grade of only six-tenths of a percent and a pushing grade of only one and a quarter percent were huge advantages over Raton Pass's steepness. The longer cutoff therefore saved time, and it quickly became, and still is, the Santa Fe's main freight route.

The Santa Fe built both small wood-frame depots and, because of anticipated traffic on the line, more elaborate masonry depots in key locations on the cutoff. The frame depots were similar to the "No. 1 Standard for Branch Lines" but with extended roof eaves and smaller windows. The reinforced concrete and stucco depots were designed by architect Myron Church. Their simplified Mission Revival style was well suited to the hot, dry climate of eastern New Mexico, with thick walls, wide overhangs to shade walls and windows, and covered, open-air waiting rooms. All were 24 feet wide, with three standard lengths: 81 feet, 93 feet (built only in Texico), and 135 feet. The basic plan consisted of a single waiting room, agent's office and freight room on the first level, and second-level living quarters, consist-

ing of either a dormitory for railroad workers or an agent's apartment. Only a few of the eleven frame depots survive, and these are used as private residences. Of the twelve Mission-style depots five survive—the public face of the Belen Cutoff.

Clovis:
Transition to Air Travel

The Eastern Railway of New Mexico, the Santa Fe subsidiary that built the Belen Cutoff, established a new town close to the Texas border and named it Riley, often referred to as Riley's Switch; as with many western town names, its origin has been lost, although there are several possible explanations. The most plausible is that the town was named for one of the Riley family, who settled the area before the railroad arrived. In any case, the name Riley was used only for a year; the railroad called its station Clovis even before the name was officially changed in 1907. Some think that Clovis, honoring a medieval French king, was chosen by the wife of Santa Fe Railway president Edward Payson Ripley, whose family had recently toured France. Others credit the daughter of chief engineer James

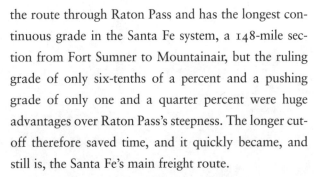

Fig. 54. Gran Quivira Hotel, Clovis, with Clovis depot in the background. Courtesy of the Museum of New Mexico, neg. no. 72668.

Dunn, who was studying French history in school.

The origin of the town itself is much clearer. In 1906, W. B. Storey, system chief engineer, directed right-of-way agent R. C. Reid to purchase the first level section of land west of Texico. While the railroad grade was surveyed, the Santa Fe planned Clovis's railyard and laid out its streets. After much controversy, when Melrose, the railroad's first choice as a division point, was eliminated for lack of water, Clovis was selected; it was also chosen to be the connection with the Pecos Valley line. As a division point, Clovis received not only the requisite railroad depot but also maintenance buildings such as a roundhouse, lodging and dining places such as the Gran Quivira Harvey House, administrative offices, a railroad hospital, and a reading room. Records from 1909 list a water tank, four wells, three water cranes, a concrete reservoir, a cinder hoist, reinforced concrete powerhouse, brick blacksmith shop, brick lavatory, reinforced concrete roundhouse with twenty-eight stalls, a 90-foot diameter turntable, and several small buildings, including a section house and bunkhouses. In 1910, a steel and brick machine shop and brick storehouse were added and the

roundhouse was enlarged. A Railroad Express Agency building was built west of the depot around 1915. Storey's letter to R. C. Reid, now in the museum in the Clovis depot, dictated the layout of the yard, with the depot and hotel on the north side of the track and the yard and roundhouse to the south.

Clovis's importance to American transportation continued when it was chosen as a stopover by the Transcontinental Air Transport Company (TAT). Teaming up with the Santa Fe and Penn Railways, the TAT sought to halve the time it took to cross the United States by incorporating air travel. The TAT's route was from Los Angeles to Clovis by plane, from Clovis to Oklahoma by rail, from Oklahoma to Ohio by plane, with a final train trip to New York City arriving on the third day, forty-eight hours later. On July 8, 1929, Charles Lindbergh flew to Clovis with Amelia Earhart as passenger, inaugurating the new venture. The TAT eventually became Trans World Airlines (TWA), and the airfield near Clovis became Cannon Air Force Base.

The Pecos subdivision was the last in the Santa Fe's system to use steam, continuing into the mid-1950s,

Fig. 55. Classification tracks, REA building, depot, and Gran Quivira Hotel, Clovis. Photo by Don Erb, courtesy of the Kansas State Historical Society, Topeka, Kansas.

but almost all of the buildings and structures that served Clovis are now gone. When the railroad demolished the freight house in the 1980s, they hauled away the large "Santa Fe: Be Safe" sign attached to the roof. Clovis residents demanded that the sign be returned; sentimentality won, and the sign still marks the former freight house location where Main Street meets the tracks. Besides the beloved sign, the other surviving railyard structures include the turntable, the foundations of the roundhouse, the railroad depot, a Harvey House, and an office building.

The railroad depot, built in 1907, is typical of the largest Eastern Railway depots, 135 feet long. Like the other eleven masonry depots on the line, it was constructed of concrete and has a pebbledash stucco finish. The Mission Revival elements at Clovis included open-air waiting rooms on either end, a tiled gable roof on both the first and second stories, and simple solid overhang brackets. As in Vaughn and Melrose, also determined to be important stops, the hexagonal agent's bay window extends to the second floor. The second-story living quarters at Clovis provided a dormitory for railroad employees, with four rooms and a bathroom on

both the west and east wings. When passenger service along the line was terminated in 1971, the depot was left vacant. It was purchased in 1989 and is now used as a model train museum. It has undergone only minor alterations, including the infill of the arches of the east-end breezeway in the 1920s. It is currently painted tan with brown trim, the 1950s paint scheme.

East of the depot is the Gran Quivira, now vacant and tangled in weeds but once a luxurious hotel operated by the Fred Harvey Company. The building, built around 1909 or 1910, was named for the ruins of an American Indian pueblo and Spanish mission twenty-five miles south of Mountainair. It was probably designed by depot architect Myron Church, and it shares Mission Revival elements with the depot, such as the tile roof (in this case a hip) with overhanging eaves and a stucco finish. But Church made grander statements in the hotel: an elegant track-facing arcade had since been enclosed, but the track-facing remate (continuation of the facade, which projects above the roofline) retains its sweeping curves and an intricate clover and triangle insert. Behind it another remate rises above the second-story roofline.

The Gran Quivira was the first hotel in Clovis to have a banquet room, which was marketed by manager John O. Pritchard to attract Clovis residents as well as tourists. This was the case with many Harvey House hotels, which became hubs of community activity. According to locals, it was "the only good place in town to eat" in the 1950s and 1960s.[3] It was a regular stop for the TAT's transcontinental passengers, providing an elegant dinner before the train ride to Oklahoma. The busboys were assigned rooms in the depot next door. A small gift shop sold newspapers, sandwiches, and postcards. By the early 1970s, the building was underutilized; the railroad used a portion for offices and rented the meeting room to Clovis community organizations. Eventually the entire building was boarded up.

In what must have been a cramped arrangement, the depot housed division offices before a division-office building was built east of the Gran Quivira in 1920. The first floor of the spacious new building had a telegrapher's office; dispatcher, trainmaster, and roadmaster offices; and file rooms. The second floor included offices for the chief clerk and superintendent, a large open space for the superintendent's clerks, and a drafting room. Less adorned than either the Gran Quivira or depot, the division-office building features some very simple Mission details such as red tile for its mansard roof, a small inset parapet, and fine wood details inside.

Clovis is still an active railyard, with seventy-five to a hundred trains passing through each day. The historic railyard structures and looming grain elevators look on as trains are reconfigured on the many classification tracks.

Melrose:
The Boomtown That Never Was

In 1905 a group of investors, including Joseph "J. L."

Fig. 56. Melrose depot, ca. 2000. Photo by author.

Downing, came to New Mexico's eastern plains to develop a new town. Downing bought out his partners when he learned of the Santa Fe's plans for the Belen Cutoff and purchased a quarter section for himself. The area was originally called Brown-Horn for its proximity to Brown's ranch, Wild Horse, and the Pig Pen Ranch owned by Lonny Horn. But when the town site was platted in February 1906, the Santa Fe Railway changed the name to Melrose for the Melrose, Ohio, location of their administrative offices.

The Santa Fe intended to use Melrose as a division point, so the depot, built in 1907, is the largest of the three Eastern Railway concrete depot standards. The railroad began building other division-point facilities, but in 1908 all construction in Melrose was halted; the railroad blamed the lack of water, a persistent problem in the arid plains, and the distance from Melrose to other towns, which was not economical for train runs. The *Portales Times* reported: "The superintendent of construction work on the eighteen-stall roundhouse and $20,000 depot in course of construction here has been wired to discontinue all work at that place. . . . The railroad company has just purchased over four hundred acres of land at Clovis at the cost of $12,000 and it is reported will immediately sink wells there for water. The location of the division point at that place will depend on the finding of a sufficient supply of water."[4] Although Melrose boasted twelve thousand residents in 1908, the population quickly shifted to Clovis.

When the railroad abandoned Melrose, it had already built foundations for several buildings, and the roundhouse had been constructed "up to the window sills," according to railroad records.[5] Only the depot was complete. Its plan, like the other Eastern Railway depots, includes a freight room on the west with the familiar small, high windows, freight doors at ground level, and a simple brick platform around the perimeter. The covered breezeway on the south end and deep roof overhangs with simple solid curved brackets provided much-needed shade for waiting passengers.

The main industries in the sleepy town, now home to only a thousand residents, are wheat and cattle, and the large depot is still used by the railroad for offices and maintenance. Dwarfed by grain towers looming to the north, it sits between a main track and siding, a picturesque reminder of a boomtown that never was.

Fort Sumner:
The Depot That Straddled Two Towns

Fort Sumner operated from 1862 to 1868, with the goal of gathering American Indians to farm the Bosque Redondo, a band of trees and fertile land along the Pecos River. The experiment was doomed from the start; various tribes were all confined to a space of forty square miles, and inevitably disputes arose. The fort was sold to Lucien Maxwell, land baron and millionaire, who used the officers' quarters as his home. It was there in Maxwell's bedroom in 1881 that Sheriff Pat Garrett killed Billy the Kid.

Nearby there was a small settlement that had

Fig. 57. Fort Sumner depot, ca. 2000. Photo by author.

applied for a post office under the name Sunnyside in 1878. When grading for the Eastern Railway reached the banks of the Pecos River early in 1905, it established a construction camp near Sunnyside, west of Truchas Creek, to build a steel bridge across the Pecos—a huge undertaking. The bridge has fifteen spans of 100 feet, with a foundation of piles driven down to solid rock, 31 feet beneath the river's surface. The camp boasted two saloons, the Prairie Dog and the Blue Goose. A little yard engine for carrying materials for the bridge construction had a number two inscribed in a circle on the front of the boiler and became known affectionately as Old Two-Spot.

When the construction camp eventually metamorphosed into a proper town, named Fort Sumner for the old military stronghold on the Bosque, the two towns coexisted. The survey for Fort Sumner followed the north boundary of the Bosque Redondo American Indian reservation, with streets oriented southeast and northwest. Sunnyside was surveyed by Charles Wesley "CW" Foor with north-south streets 50 feet wide. The dividing line between the two towns was Fort Sumner Avenue, now U.S. Highway 60.

In 1908 a depot was constructed to serve both Fort Sumner and Sunnyside. Although both towns were eager for more railroad facilities, the Santa Fe put its larger operations in Vaughn, and Fort Sumner/Sunnyside received the smallest of the three standard masonry depot sizes. The same structure was built in Encino, Willard, Mountainair, Becker, Gallaher, La Lande, and Ricardo. The freight room is on the northwest, next to an agent's bay with stairs to the dormitory-style living quarters above. The single waiting room opens to a breezeway on the southeast end. The freight doors are at railcar height, with a loading platform on the northwest end. A chimney with a double flue once exhausted the agent's bay and upstairs apartment's woodstoves, at the time the only source of heat. The hexagonal agent's bay which, unlike the larger versions of the Eastern Railway depot did not extend to the second story, surveys the main track to the northeast, but there is also a siding to the southwest; the depot is trackbound. When the station was new, it had the typical identification signage on either end, except that passengers approaching from the west were greeted with the name Sunnyside and those from the east with Fort Sumner. This confusing situation would soon change.

On July 3, 1908, only two days after regular train service was introduced, the area was hit by a tornado. Most of the vicinity was destroyed, nearly all the sheep in Roosevelt County were killed, and women and children were sent up to the depot for safety; as the only structure that was made of concrete, it was the safest place in either town. The aftermath of the tornado strained the finances of both local governments. Nearly a year later, on April 17, 1909, officials from Sunnyside and Fort Sumner decided to share police duties, taxation, water distribution, and other town functions. They united under the name Fort Sumner, and Sunnyside became the Sunnyside Addition.

People in Fort Sumner, as it has been called since 1938, still remember that the railroad depot was integral to the community. The train brought the mail, sometimes stopping to deliver the sack, sometimes throwing it to a catcher with a hook on a post, and sometimes dropping it, scattering mail along the tracks. People often went up to the station simply to watch the three or four daily passenger trains stop to take on riders. The last station agent at Fort Sumner was John Brown, who loved his position so much that the community called him Mr. Santa Fe.

Vaughn:
Parched in the Plains

The Stinson Cattle Trail, from Texas to New Mexico's Estancia Valley, was blazed in 1882 by Jim Stinson, manager of the New Mexico Land and Livestock Company. He drove twenty thousand cattle in eight separate herds to supply western forts, with an important stop at what is now Vaughn. The Santa Fe Railway chose the same stop for a division point on their Belen Cutoff line, naming it for railroad civil engineer Major G. W. Vaughn.

At Vaughn the Belen Cutoff crossed existing El Paso & Southwestern tracks that linked El Paso with Dalhart, Texas. The cutoff was built toward Vaughn from both the east and west, reaching the town from the west in 1905 and from the east in 1907. A high-level crossing was constructed and a turntable was built in 1907. The following year, the railroad built a roundhouse and a depot, the largest of the standard masonry designs. In 1910, it constructed a reading room for railroad employees.

The depot's two-story agent's bay observes the

Fig. 58. Vaughn depot, 2001. Photo by Glen Gollrad.

tracks of the still-busy freight route to the north. The building once shared its subtle Mission Revival elements—gabled tile roof, arched open-air waiting room, and solid brackets—and its trackside site with the Las Chaves Harvey House. The hotel, built the same year, also shared the depot's designer, Santa Fe staff architect Myron Church. With its shaded arcade facing the tracks, the elegant Harvey House was an oasis in the desert, offering delicacies such as homemade ice cream. When Charles Lindbergh's plane experienced engine failure in 1928 and he was forced to land near Vaughn, he ate all of his meals in the Las Chaves dining room.

Despite its division-point status, Vaughn was plagued by a lack of water. The Santa Fe built two underground concrete cisterns and a steel water tank in 1908. Water for the reading room, hotel, and depot was hauled in tank cars from Willard and Negra. The El Paso & Southwestern's water came from a pipeline to Bonito Creek in Lincoln County a hundred miles away. In late 1909, the Santa Fe signed a contract with the other railroad to siphon water off the pipe into one of its reservoirs at a rate of 24¢ per thousand gallons. This water was for the repair shops and steam engines.

In 1936, eight years after Lindbergh's visit, the

Harvey House closed, and eventually it and the other railyard facilities were demolished. Only the Vaughn depot remains. The town is still at a transportation crossroads, at the intersection of two important freight railroads and U.S. Highways 54, 60, and 285.

Mountainair: Trackbound in the Pinto Bean Capital of the World

The town site of Mountainair was developed in the early 1900s by Colonel E. C. Manning; John W. Corbett, a newspaperman from Winfield, Kansas; and E. S. Stover, former Kansas governor. Seeking to cash in on the Santa Fe Railway's rumored plans to build the Belen Cutoff through the area, they applied for a post office in 1903. Due to delay in construction of the cutoff, mail was carried three times a week from Albuquerque. When the line was finally completed in 1908, a railroad station was built and the town thrived. The first station agent was J. J. "Bill" White; his wife operated the telegraph.

Situated at the end of Main Street in Mountainair amid vacant, red-painted bean elevators and old boarding houses, the Mountainair depot is today a well-preserved example of the smallest of the Eastern Railway's masonry standards. The first floor of the 81-foot-long depot includes a waiting room, agent's office, baggage room, and freight room. The baggage and freight rooms, with a railcar-level loading platform, were relatively large due to high freight traffic through Mountainair, where prolific bean harvests gave the area the nickname the Pinto Bean Capital of the World. The agent's bay overlooks the main line to the southeast, but there is also siding to the northwest. The curved metal letters of the station sign echo the arches of the shady breezeway, which functioned as an outdoor waiting area. The second floor, with two bed-

Fig. 59. Mountainair depot, ca. 1996. Photo by author.

Fig. 60. Mountainair depot, ca. 1915. Courtesy of the Museum of New Mexico, neg. no. 65636.

rooms and a bath, was used for living quarters from 1944 until the early 1950s, when Mountainair had grown enough that the station agent could find housing in town. It was then used as centralized traffic control (CTC) dispatching system offices.

Like many New Mexican towns, Mountainair suffered from a lack of water, and the water that was available, from the railroad's well, was so alkaline that the railroad eventually abandoned it and refilled its tanks at Willard. Persistent drought in the 1950s destroyed the bean crop and nearly devastated the town. Today Mountainair is a quiet community; the depot and bean elevators are vestiges of its past as a center of commerce.

Pecos Valley Branch: The Peavine

In the late nineteenth century, open land in the West was available to entrepreneurs who tried to tame the harsh landscape and make their fortunes. The Pecos Valley, in the isolated eastern Llano Estacado "staked" plains, had its share of impediments to development, including a lack of water. In 1886, a year known as the Big Die, a drought killed 35 percent of the cattle in the region. The next year, Charles

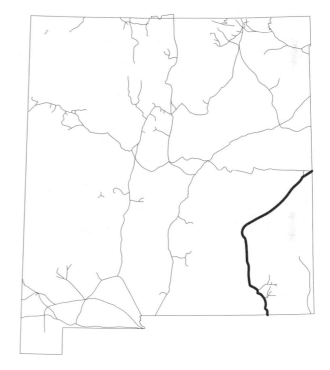

B. Eddy, who had owned a cattle ranch in the Pecos Valley with his brother John since 1884, formed the Pecos Valley Land and Ditch Company to build a diversion ditch on the Pecos River. The following year, promoter Charles Greene and famous Lincoln County former sheriff Pat Garrett (who owned land near Roswell) joined him to solve the area's ongoing drought problems by providing irrigation. They also planned to plat a townsite and sell lots.

One of the investors secured by Greene was a cigar manufacturer from Chicago, Robert Weems Tansill. Tansill, a former resident of Colorado Springs, introduced Eddy to James John "J. J." Hagerman, who had made his fortune in Michigan iron mines, then retired to Colorado, where he hoped the climate would cure his tuberculosis. At the time Hagerman had already been involved in both silver- and gold-mining operations and had built and sold the 238-mile Colorado Midland Railroad running from Colorado Springs to Aspen. The agricultural potential of the Pecos Valley interested Hagerman, but he realized that success depended on a means of importing and exporting goods into the area. In 1889, Hagerman became a partner in the newly established Pecos Irrigation and Improvement Company to build irrigation projects such as canals, dams, and reservoirs and construct a railroad from Pecos, Texas (a station on the Texas & Pacific) north into New Mexico.

In 1890, the irrigation company built many of its canals, Avalon Dam, and the crucial structure in the irrigation system—a wooden flume built by the Witt Brothers to carry the canal across the Pecos River. Also in 1890, the Pecos Valley Railway, advertising itself as the "Fruit Belt Route," was formed with the goal of shipping cattle to the South and fruits and vegetables to southern Texas. The fruit the railroad hoped to ship included sugar beets, which had been planted in the valley as an agricultural experiment. The railroad became operational in 1891, linking the new town of Eddy to Pecos, Texas, and beyond. The timing of these ventures was poor, however. Investor funding declined after the Panic of 1893, and in July and August the Pecos River flooded, destroying the dam and wooden flume (replaced in 1903 by a concrete version that is still in use). The sugar beets failed, as did other experimental crops. The railroad line reached only as far as Eddy until 1894, when it was extended another seventy miles to the established community of Roswell. Like its predecessor, the Goodnight-Loving cattle trail, it followed the route of the Pecos River. Cattleman Charles Goodnight called the Pecos region the "Graveyard of Hope." With continued financial strain and a falling out with Hagerman, Eddy left the partnership and moved to El Paso in 1895; Hagerman became the sole owner.

Hagerman also wanted out of the losing venture and sought to build up his railroad enough to make it salable to an established company; the natural choice was the Santa Fe, already a significant presence in New Mexico. He reorganized the company as the Pecos Valley and Northeastern Railway in 1897, and with financial help from the Santa Fe, construction began on April 14, 1898 to extend the line from Roswell to Texico, on the Texas border, and then west to connect with the Santa Fe in Amarillo. The railroad, already plagued by problems, was in chaos during the construction of the remaining 208 miles. The Santa Fe hired Mallory, Cushing & Company exclusively to grade the road and lay tracks on the entire line, although its standard practice was to divide construction into segments and use several contractors. Without enough workers on the project, construction was slow and workmanship was poor. In late September, Hagerman's own crews took over track-laying duties while Mallory, Cushing continued to grade. Hagerman, once forty miles behind the graders, caught up, even though his crew had to repair the poorly prepared grade in addition to laying track.

When the line was finally complete in early 1899, the Santa Fe purchased the Pecos Valley & Northeastern (its letters, PV&NE, earning it the nickname Peavine) from Hagerman for $2,675,902. The Peavine provided an important feeder from Attica, Kansas, through Amarillo to Pecos, Texas. In 1901, the Santa Fe formally integrated the Peavine into its system by acquiring most of the stock in order to prevent another company from gaining control. As passenger traffic increased, the Santa Fe began building railroad depots for the line. The company built in a utilitarian adaptation of Mission Revival style, by that time identified with the Santa Fe in the West, exemplified by the Portales and Artesia depots. The Carlsbad and Roswell depots, initially handsome brick structures with hipped roofs, were remodeled in a Pueblo Revival style. The passenger portion of the Roswell depot was destroyed by fire in 2001; now only the freight portion remains. Two frame depots from the line, at Elida (a "Frame Depot No. 4 for Branch Lines") and Kenna (a "Frame Depot No. 3 for Branch Lines"), are used as private residences and have been extensively altered. Another tiny frame depot that served Orla and Angeles, Texas, and Loving, New Mexico, is vacant and located on a ranch in Carlsbad. These seven depots are all that remain of the eighteen depots that the Santa Fe built after purchasing the line; no Pecos Valley Railroad depots remain.

Hagerman died in Rome in 1909, but he left the railroad as his legacy. The line is still active, used primarily to

Fig. 61. Loving depot, 1996. Photo by author.

haul potash and sulphur, discovered in the Permian Basin east of Carlsbad in 1925; there is no passenger service.

Loving:
Depot on the Move

The tiny depot on a ranch on Standpipe Road in southern Carlsbad was originally built by the Santa Fe to serve Orla, Texas, in 1910. The Santa Fe had taken over the Peavine in 1901 and built several depots along the line.

The tiny 12- by 40-foot wood-frame building was designed to be moved easily as needed. The station at Orla was closed in 1926, and nine years later the depot moved six miles north along the same line, to serve Angeles, Texas. In 1946 it was moved north another twenty-nine miles to Loving, New Mexico.

Loving was named for its location on the Goodnight-Loving cattle trail, a route followed by the southern part of the Peavine. Charles Goodnight and Oliver Loving began driving cattle north along the Pecos River in 1866. The Santa Fe retired the depot in 1969, after which it was moved to Carlsbad and is now vacant. The yellow paint is the Santa Fe's colonial yellow and the rectangular agent's bay is typical of the company's smaller, later depots.

Carlsbad:
The Pearl of the Pecos

Charles Eddy and his partners selected a riverside site as the headquarters for their Pecos Valley Land and Ditch Company. They celebrated their choice of location, along the south bank of the Pecos at Loving Bend, on September 15, 1888. The intent was to irrigate the area, promote agriculture and settlement, and connect it with Texas by rail. Lots were sold for $50, with a restriction against the sale, distribution, and manufacture of liquor. Eddy wanted to call the town Halagueño, Spanish for "alluring," after the ranch he had established with his brother in 1884. His partner Tansill, who also planned and named many of the streets, convinced him the word was too difficult to pronounce and flatteringly suggested that it should be called Eddy.

By 1889, the first school was built on South Main, and Tansill introduced Eddy to J. J. Hagerman, one of the wealthiest men in the world, who would finance Eddy's grand plans. The town was calling itself the "Pearl of the Pecos," although construction on the promised railroad did not begin until later that year. The *Eddy Argus* commented sarcastically on the railroad's progress on October 19: "It is within the range of possibilities that the whistle of a locomotive will be heard within the Pecos Valley." A year later possibility had become probability; in November 1890, the newspaper noted that "the whole of the ample riverfront has been reserved for railroad purposes, side tracks, depot, etc." The first train arrived a few months later, on January 10, 1891. The *Argus* recorded the delight of Eddy residents: "A special train pulled into this place and the whistling of the locomo-

Fig. 62. Carlsbad depot, 2001. Photo by Glen Gollrad.

tive, the firing of anvils, cheers of hundreds of citizens who had gathered at the foot of Greene St. to welcome the party, proved exciting indeed." [6]

Typically, rowdiness followed the railroad, but since Eddy was a dry town, the community of Phenix, consisting mostly of saloons, gambling halls, and houses of prostitution, developed just south of Eddy in 1892. Phenix withered when Eddy's prohibition ended in 1895, the same year Charles Eddy dissolved his partnership with Hagerman and moved to El Paso to begin new ventures.

Eddy's first depot, a frame structure (now gone), was built in 1896. With the Santa Fe's plans to link up the Peavine to its Belen Cutoff line, it was replaced in 1904 with a brick county-seat depot with a pitched roof, similar to one built the next year in Roswell. The structure was extended in 1914 and then completely rebuilt in 1929. The gabled roof was removed and replaced with a flat, parapeted roof, and the footprint was enlarged. The new Pueblo Revival style was accomplished with light-colored stucco over the brick, a small curve on the trackside parapet, and decorative vigas projecting from the stucco on each facade. In 1972, a detached freight house was built just south of the depot, and many of the square portal openings and freight-room doors on both trackside and streetside were infilled. A vestige of the semicircular arched window of the original brick depot is visible through the open portal south of the agent's bay, which faces the tracks and river beyond to the east.

Even after Eddy moved on and Hagerman sold his railroad to the Santa Fe, Tansill lived in Eddy until his death in 1902. It was his suggestion to change the town's name to Carlsbad, to invoke the famous Karlsbad Springs in Czechoslovakia and thereby promote the springs, located two-and-a-half miles to the north. These were celebrated for their high mineral content and "noted all over the West," as detailed in the *Young Observer* in December of 1902, "for the great medicinal properties of its waters in cases of stomach trouble, constipation or liver troubles."[7] The town was officially renamed Carlsbad on May 23, 1899. In the 1920s, Carlsbad's tourism industry was solidified with the development of Carlsbad Caverns as an attraction. When European potash, used in fertilizers, became unavailable in 1939, the U.S. Potash Company expanded its mines east of Carlsbad. Potash shipments made Carlsbad the second largest revenue-producing station on the Santa Fe's system in the mid-1950s. From its inception as a railroad town without a railroad, to a mecca for health seekers, stopover for tourists, and then mining center, Carlsbad has adapted and thrives.

Artesia:
The Town with Many Names

In 1866 cattle baron John Chisum blazed the Chisum Trail, moving his longhorns from Paris in eastern Texas into southeastern New Mexico. His route

Fig. 63. Streetside view of Artesia depot, 2003. Photo by author.

passed through the dry Pecos Valley; water was rare, but there was an artesian spring at Blake's Spring, a stop on a local stage line. Artesian springs, named for Artois in France (called Artesium in Roman times), have internal pressure that makes them flow spontaneously. Blake's Spring also became a regular stop on the Chisum Trail where the cattle stopped to drink. It came to be known as Chisum Spring Camp or South Chisum Camp, for the famous cattle drive.

Eventually the Pecos Valley Railroad, which had been stalled in Eddy, made its way north. The railroad, recognizing the importance of the springs, built a siding and called it Miller, but when the community applied for a post office four years later, they requested the name Stegman to pay tribute to early settlers. That name never stuck, and the town continued to be known as Miller until 1903. That year, John Richey, an enterprising Kansan, purchased land in the area and sold home sites; to promote settlement, he celebrated the town's greatest asset, naming his community Artesia. The name was formally adopted on January 1, 1904. The springs, so valuable in the desert Southwest, later led to the discovery of oil, an

Fig. 64.
Trackside
agent's bay,
Artesia depot,
2001. Photo
by Glen
Gollrad.

even rarer resource.

Artesia's railroad depot has a less convoluted past than its name. The structure was built by the Santa Fe around 1912 to replace a frame depot built by the Pecos Valley Railroad in 1897 that was then converted to a freight depot (since destroyed). The depot shares much with the Santa Fe's county-seat depots that were built on the railroad's western lines, but with a stucco finish rather than traditional brick. The structure also borrows Mission Revival elements of the Belen Cutoff design, with the familiar pitched red clay-tile roof and curvilinear parapets. It has only one story, however; by this time housing station agents was no longer an issue, and second-story apartments were eliminated from the Santa Fe's floor plans. Unique features at Artesia include brick quoins that mark the building's corners, a brick coping, and brick

detail around arches and window openings. Brick even outlines the Santa Fe's familiar cross-in-circle logo. The elongated As of the whimsical station sign, lettered in a style not seen in other Santa Fe buildings, mirror the Roman arch of the agent's bay window.

The Artesia depot has been renovated and is now a chamber of commerce and visitor center. The arches of the summer waiting room on the south end, once walled in, are now enclosed with glass to recall the former arcade. The long north-side freight extension and loading platform, added when the freight depot was retired in 1940, face the tracks to the east. Artesia is a community that has always recognized and developed its assets; it is blessed with water, oil, and a unique, historic depot.

Portales:
Adjacent Icehouse

The Portales springs were well known before the arrival of the railroad as a source of water in the dry eastern plains. The name Portales, Spanish for "porches," references the overhanging cliff formations that resemble the porches of traditional adobe houses. The area was undeveloped with the exception of a one-room supply store operated by "Uncle" Josh Morrison.

The Pecos Valley & Northeastern extended the Peavine line from Roswell in 1899, and a construction camp was established near the springs. Morrison moved his store to the camp on skids, and railroad promoter J. J. Hagerman attracted homesteaders with the promise of abundant water. Though he could not deliver his promise in a region plagued by drought, the town grew anyway. The railroad built a board and batten depot in 1901. As rumors of the Santa Fe's Belen Cutoff circulated, the city fathers of Portales were confident that the cutoff would cross the Peavine

Fig. 65. Portales depot, ca. 2001. Photo by author.

at their town, providing an important junction. They balked, however, at what the railroad required for this honor: $50,000 and forty acres of land. The Santa Fe built through Texico instead, then constructed a spur from Cameo on the Peavine so that the connection with the cutoff was now in Clovis.

In 1913, a new brick county-seat depot replaced the earlier frame building (now gone). Construction funds were raised through popular subscription, and a site east of the existing depot at the end of Avenue A was chosen. The site's owner, Sam Nixon, put in $50 of his own. Constructed by contractor A. McLeod for $11,102.77, the depot was the brother of depots in Hagerman (demolished sometime after 1971), Las Cruces, and other locations in Oklahoma, Kansas, and Colorado. Normally the brick was left exposed, but in New Mexico the railroad evoked Mission Revival style with a coat of pebbledash stucco and a red-tile roof. Details include the Santa Fe logo incorporated into the concrete coping of the parapeted ends and an elegant quatrefoil formed into the stucco

over the agent's bay. As in Las Cruces, the open-air waiting room was eliminated in favor of a longer freight room. Also like Las Cruces, the passenger portion of the building has a gable roof with parapeted ends, and the freight portion, at ground level rather than raised to railcar level, has a flat roof with an articulated parapet. A rectangular agent's bay surveys the main track to the northwest.

In the mid-1920s, railroad workers planted and maintained a small park adjacent to the depot with shady black locust trees and grass that attracted not only travelers but also Portales residents, who gathered there to engage in a favorite pastime: watching the trains. This and a coal-loading chute once located along the tracks between the station and Main Street are both gone.

Adjacent to the depot on the east side of Avenue A is one of the only remaining icehouses in New Mexico. The handsome brick warehouse was added to an earlier block structure in 1928 by brothers-in-law Luther Thomas and James Lee; in addition to providing ice for homes and businesses in Portales, it also sometimes made three-hundred-pound blocks to be loaded into the train's refrigerator cars, called reefers. The icehouse is now a sign shop and is being restored. Next door, the tiny depot, dwarfed by grain towers, is trackbound by the main line and an active siding, a serious impediment to reuse.

New Mexico Central

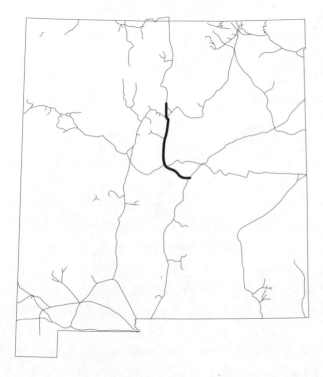

Frances Torrance and William Andrews, financial investors from Pennsylvania, incorporated the Santa Fe, Albuquerque & Pacific Railroad Company in 1900 with the ambitious goal of building to the West Coast. This plan was soon abandoned in favor of connecting to the El Paso & Rock Island Railway, a subsidiary of the El Paso & Northeastern, to provide a link to New Mexico's territorial capital. The name of the railroad was changed to Santa Fe Central Railway,

and a junction was planned, to be called Torrance after the railroad's founder. The Santa Fe Central was completed in August 1903, with the last spike set at Kennedy. The Santa Fe Central then built several simple depots, with gable roofs, slight overhangs, and rectangular agent's bays incorporating the telegraph pole and semaphore. Corrugated metal siding, stamped to look like clapboard, and corrugated metal roofs protected the wood structures from sparks created by passing trains.

A few years later, the same partners formed the Albuquerque Eastern Railway to build a branch to Albuquerque from their stop at Calvert. Construction began in 1908 but was never completed, reaching only a little farther than Frost, about halfway. This and the line from Torrance to Santa Fe were consolidated the same year and renamed New Mexico Central Railroad. With only a minor change to Railway in 1918 and since it had been known as the Santa Fe Central for only five years, the line came to be known as the New Mexico Central, even after it was purchased by the Santa Fe in 1926 for $700,000.

The Santa Fe inherited the line's water problems and lack of traffic. There was no water supply between Santa Fe and Otto, forty-four miles to the south, and water was carried in tank cars. However, there was also too much water in the form of heavy rains and melting snow, which softened the dirt ballast and spread the rails. The Santa Fe operated the New Mexico Central as a minor branch with self-propelled passenger cars called doodlebugs. In 1928, it began abandoning trackage. The Kennedy to Santa Fe segment was the first to be retired. The next year, the Torrance to Estancia portion was eliminated. By 1943, all that remained was the short twenty-eight- mile run from Calvert to Estancia. By then Calvert was known as Moriarty for a local ranch owner; the Moriarty-Estancia spur operated until 1974.

There were once nine depots on the New Mexico Central route. The depots at Torrance, Calvert, Stanley, and Bianca were built by the Santa Fe Central in 1903. The Torrance depot was retired in 1954, the two-story passenger portion was removed four years later, and the freight portion now provides hay storage on a ranch in Torrance. The Calvert (Moriarty) depot was retired in 1949 and remains on its original site but has been unrecognizably altered. The Bianca, Stanley, McIntosh, and Willard depots, retired in the late 1920s and early 1930s as the lines were abandoned, have been demolished. The depot in McIntosh that now serves as a residence is not the McIntosh depot but was moved from Los Cerrillos. The only depot built by the Santa Fe Central that remains in good condition is the Santa Fe depot, now a restaurant.

Other depots on the line were provided by the Santa Fe, which took over the line in 1926. The Kennedy depot was built in 1907 for the town at the intersection of the Santa Fe's main line and the Santa Fe Central; it was relocated to Eldorado and is used as an office. The Estancia depot, which replaced an earlier Santa Fe Central structure, sits vacant on a ranch south of town.

Estancia:
The Moveable Depot

The town of Estancia borrowed its name, Spanish for "resting place," from a nearby spring. Its first station was a simple Santa Fe Central depot built in 1903, before the railroad consolidated with the Albuquerque Eastern to become the New Mexico Central. Its sheet-

Fig. 66. Estancia depot, ca. 1996. Photo by author.

metal siding, stamped to look like clapboard, protected the main structure from sparks created by passing trains.

The Santa Fe Railway took over the New Mexico Central's lines in 1926 and in 1951 replaced the original depot (now gone) with a 16- by 40-foot depot, which originally served the Belen Cutoff town of Lucy, a minor stop. The depot was built by the Santa Fe's subsidiary Eastern Railway of New Mexico in 1908. It was typical of the cutoff's frame depots, which foreshadowed the simplified details of the Santa Fe's standard "Frame Depot No. 1 for Branch Lines" issued in 1910. Features included a hexagonal bay window tucked under the roofline and minimal roof brackets. Of the eleven frame depots built on the Belen Cutoff, it is the only one that remains.

The depot was retired from Lucy in 1938 and was finally moved to Estancia thirteen years later. By 1951, the New Mexico Central had been reduced to a short segment from Moriarty to Estancia, and the tiny depot was at the end of the line until the station closed in 1969. It was then purchased for $1,000 by a local rancher, who moved it to his land south of town.

Fig. 67. Streetside view of Santa Fe Central/Chile Line depot, 1996. Photo by author.

Fig. 68. Santa Fe Central/Chile Line depot, streetside waiting-room door, ca. 2001. Photo by Sharon Wharton.

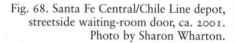

Santa Fe:
Union Depot—The Santa Fe Central
and the Chile Line

The brick depot on Guadalupe Street in Santa Fe is known for its use by the Denver & Rio Grande, but the depot was actually built by the Santa Fe Central late in 1903. Earlier that year, it completed its branch from Torrance, a stop on the El Paso & Northeastern Railroad, to Santa Fe, connecting with the Denver & Rio Grande's line to Colorado (formerly Texas, Santa Fe & Northern tracks to Española but acquired by the Rio Grande in 1895).

In 1906, the Santa Fe Central and Rio Grande signed an agreement to jointly use the depot, and the Rio Grande converted its two-story frame depot (constructed by the Texas, Santa Fe & Northern) to an icehouse. The structure, built in 1887, was located on the other side of the Santa Fe River south of Catron Street and east of the Denver & Rio Grande's wye. It was later demolished.

The Eastern Brick–style depot was the only masonry structure built by the Santa Fe Central. Its construction was not warranted by the small amount of traffic, but because of an intense rivalry with the Santa Fe Railway, operating in the same railyard, the Santa Fe Central built a sturdy, handsome structure. The building has a clay-tile hipped roof with flared eaves, brick walls, and no brackets. A freight room separated the two waiting rooms, an unusual layout. Now that the depot is used as a restaurant, the original floor plan is muddled, and several additions have buried the hexagonal agent's bay inside the building. It once faced the tracks to the east and can still be seen near the restaurant's hostess station. A corresponding rectangular projection on Guadalupe Street once accommodated the depot's restrooms.

The Santa Fe Central was reorganized as the New Mexico Central in 1908, and until 1926, when the Santa Fe Railway acquired the New Mexico Central's lines, it continued to share the depot with the Rio Grande. Since the Santa Fe already had a Santa Fe station, the depot was used exclusively by the Denver & Rio Grande until 1941, when the Chile Line was abandoned.

Western Division of the Atlantic & Pacific: The Fourth Transcontinental Railroad

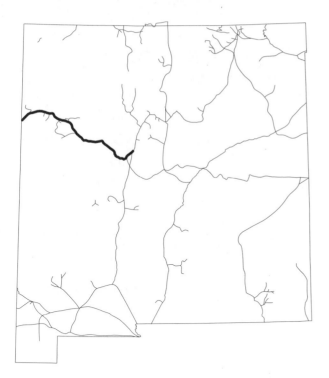

In 1866, John C. Fremont, formerly of the Kansas Pacific, formed the Atlantic & Pacific Railroad Company to build a railroad from Missouri to the West Coast. The residents of Springfield optimistically welcomed the president and directors of the A&P when the track arrived on May 3, 1870, with a speech by John S. Phelps. "You can hardly appreciate the difficulties under which we have labored, without an easy and expeditious connection with other portions of the State," he said.

> We were in an almost isolated condition; access to our country could only be obtained by days of tiresome and weary travel, over rough and rugged roads,and through a hilly and mountainous country. . . . This is an event which opens to us a new and a bright future henceforward, by reason of an easy and rapid communication with all parts of our country. . . . This road is to be the great thoroughfare to the Pacific. . . . No trans-continental route possesses the advantages this route possesses. . . . But when this road shall be extended to the Pacific, the products of India and Japan will pass our very doors on their way to St. Louis and other portions of our country.[8]

But by 1873, the railroad having been bankrupted by the Civil War, only 327 miles had been constructed. Through the Tripartite Agreement of 1880, the Santa Fe Railway and the St. Louis & San Francisco (known as the Frisco) agreed to share ownership and stock of the failing company. In 1881, they began building track west from the Santa Fe's main line at a location dubbed A&P Junction. Late in 1883, the last spike was driven at "the Needles," a new California railroad settlement near the Arizona border named for sharp peaks nearby. This connected the line to the Southern Pacific and formed the fourth transcontinental railroad in the United States. Like the other three, the Thirty-fifth Parallel Trans Continental Line basically followed the original surveys commissioned by the U.S. government in 1853. The Santa Fe Pacific Railroad, a subsidiary of the Santa Fe, acquired the Atlantic & Pacific's Western Division in 1897, and the Santa Fe absorbed the line five years later.

Several branches were built off of the Western Division of the A&P in New Mexico, including logging branches to access timber in the Zuni Mountains and spurs to reach coalfields north of Gallup. In the 1950s, lines were built to newly discovered uranium deposits; these were abandoned when nuclear power became unpopular.

Currently only three significant structures remain on the line in New Mexico. The Gallup depot is a large Pueblo Revival station, and the Grants depot is a small frame structure. The Laguna Pueblo depot, where the train once stopped so that tourists could buy American Indian handcrafts and jewelry, was retired when the tracks were rerouted in 1909. Purchased in 1917 for $250, it was remodeled long ago as a private residence.

Gallup:

Pueblo Revival in American Indian Country

The Blue Goose Saloon and General Store, located near the Arizona border, was a stop for the Pony Express stagecoach with access to Chaco, Acoma Pueblo, and the Painted Desert. When the Western Division of the Atlantic & Pacific built tracks through the area in 1881, the stagecoach stop became a viable town. It was known as Gallup for A&P paymaster David Gallup, because railroad workers went to "Gallup's" on payday to collect their earnings.

Located at the center of the Gallup-Zuni coalfield, part of the huge San Juan Basin coalfield, the area produced more coal than anywhere else in New Mexico from 1886 to 1903; however, the inferior coal

Fig. 69. Trackside view of Gallup depot, 2004. Photo by author.

burned poorly, causing large, hot cinders to issue from the stacks, a fire hazard.

Gallup was chosen as a division point in 1895 and once had a full complement of shops and repair facilities. The depot and El Navajo Harvey House, replacing a frame depot/hotel, were designed in 1916 by the Harvey Company's Mary Colter; the project was her first as chief designer. Both were built concurrently but were not completed until 1923 because of World War I. The official opening day was May 23; the Harvey Company arranged an American Indian ceremony to bless the new hotel. Unlike Colter's earlier Mission Revival designs, this later building was a tribute to the American Indian: a huge Pueblo Revival structure with thick walls and inset windows, a flat roof, stepped parapets, and abstracted Pueblo-style massing. The two-story depot was made of concrete, and, at over 16,000 square feet, provided space not only for passenger waiting and ticket purchases but also for railroad operations, a telegraph office, and a Railway Express Agency. The station name and Santa Fe logo were formed into the stucco. The hotel section to the west was among the grandest in the Harvey system, with a Pueblo Revival earth-toned interior and American Indian artwork throughout, including Navajo sand paintings. It became a training ground for other large Harvey hotels in the system; many Harvey Girl waitresses settled in Gallup.

The El Navajo was also an important hub of the Harvey Company's Indian Detours. Passengers could purchase tickets that included a stopover in Gallup, and the tour company offered one-, two- and three-day guided trips into American Indian country. The Great Depression of the 1930s caused the company to cancel trips from Gallup; the Harvey House closed and was demolished in 1957.

The depot, however, has been renovated; back to its original grey color with its wooden benches polished, it is sandwiched between tracks to the north and Railroad Avenue (Route 66) to the south. Farther down the tracks is a brick repair shop, which is the only reminder of what was once a busy division point.

Fig. 70. Grants depot, ca. 1996. Photo by author.

Grants:
Named for the Railroad Contractors
Who Built the Line

The three Grant Brothers, Angus, Lewis, and John, moved from Canada to Kansas in the 1860s to become railroad contractors; they subsequently built many railroads in the West. In 1880, they began construction on the Western Division of the Atlantic & Pacific line from Isleta, New Mexico (on the Santa Fe's main line) to Needles, California. West of Laguna Pueblo, they established a construction site known as Grant's Camp. The camp received a coaling station and depot and in 1880 a post office under the name Grant. The locals, however, continued to call the town Grantes, the Spanish plural, since there were three brothers. In 1935, its name was officially changed to

Grants to reflect the local preference. Despite the origins of the town's name, the Grant brothers spent most of their time in Albuquerque, where they owned a newspaper, waterworks, the local electric utility, and the Grants Opera.

Though Grants had cycles of prosperity and hardship, logging provided an income for many residents. George Breece began lumber operations in Zuni Canyon in the late 1920s. He built a railroad, as well as an engine house and company housing, in what was known as Breecetown on the west side of Grants. Logging continued until 1941. Diamond G Lumber has absorbed the engine house, and the decaying company houses are vacant next door.

The railroad depot in Grants is one of only a few frame depots of its type; others are located in Pinole and Rialto, California. The simplified style features a gable roof spanning between stepped, parapeted wing walls and a rectangular agent's bay tucked under a shed roof. Horizontal asbestos shingle siding was added during a later remodeling. Though its construction date is unknown, clues to the depot's age include the original clapboard siding, barely seen beneath the shingles on one corner, and station agents' freight-room signatures—one reads "EML 1940 1944." Inside, high up on an old brick chimney, is the hole where the pipe of a coal stove once connected, which dates from sometime before 1929 when the station was electrified and plumbed. Across the main tracks to the south is a small brick toolhouse with a corrugated metal roof. Its construction date is also a mystery.

Silver City Branches

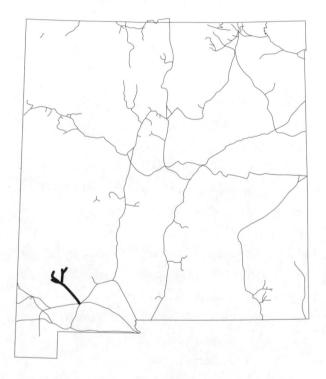

In 1882, the Silver City, Deming & Pacific Railroad was incorporated by a group of local merchants and mine owners. By 1883, the railroad connected Silver City to Deming at the intersection of the Santa Fe and Southern Pacific lines. After construction, the company accepted its lack of experience in railroad operations and leased the line to the Santa Fe.

In 1891, the Santa Fe incorporated a subsidiary, the Silver City & Northern Railroad, to build to other area mines. Splitting off the line at Whitewater, a branch was constructed through Hurley and Bayard to Hanover in 1892. In 1898, under the name Santa Rita Railroad, the Santa Fe extended the line three miles from Hanover to the Santa Rita Copper Mines. The following year, Santa Fe subsidiary Hanover Railroad built from Hanover again, to Fierro's iron, copper, and zinc mines. The Santa Fe acquired its subsidiaries in 1900; ninety years later, the Southwestern Railroad purchased most of the Santa Fe's Silver City branches. The only line still operated by the Santa Fe is the segment from Deming to Whitewater. Service to Silver City ended in 1983, and the handsome Mission Revival depot there was subsequently demolished.

The only structures left in the Santa Rita branches are the Santa Fe's wood-frame depots in Hurley, Bayard, and Whitewater (now a private residence, relocated to Central in 1970).

Hurley:
A Company Town Devoted to Copper

Named to honor Santa Fe Railway general manager J. E. Hurley, the town of Hurley was born in 1892 with the arrival of the Silver City & Northern Railroad, a Santa Fe subsidiary. The railroad was built to access the Santa Rita copper deposits, first mined in 1800 by Spanish soldier Colonel José Manuel Carrasco. The mines were operated by J. Parker Whitney from 1886 until 1900, when he sold them to the Santa Rita Mining Company, a group of New York investors. Until about 1910, the copper at Santa Rita was mined underground, but as the high-grade ores played out, Santa Rita was sold to John Sully, who formed the Chino Copper Company. He

Fig. 71. Hurley depot, 2001. Photo by author.

employed an open-pit and steam-shovel method and dynamited the earth to reach the copper deposits.

In 1911, a mill was constructed at Hurley, and the railroad became an important connection between the mines and the Hurley complex. The Santa Fe built a depot in 1911, a variation of the "Frame Depot No. 4 for Branch Lines" from the railroad's "1910 Standards." Features include clapboard siding, a gabled roof with bracketed ends, and a small single-sided hexagonal bay overlooking the main tracks to the west. To accommodate large quantities of ore, the freight room was extended by 40 feet in 1918, but otherwise there have been few changes. Inside, the original cabinets, wood floor, board and bead walls, double-hung windows, and five-panel doors remain. The exterior paint scheme was once the Santa Fe's colonial yellow with green trim.

After years of mergers and consolidations, Kennecott Copper Corporation acquired the Chino Copper Company and its Santa Rita mines in June 1933. Hurley became the location of the primary crusher and concentrator for Santa Rita's ore when Kennecott constructed a smelter in 1939 and a fire refin-ery in 1942. Residents began to experience respiratory problems, and as local Larry Himes recalled, automobile paint jobs "went bad within two years. We accepted [these things] as part of living in Hurley."[9] With the Clean Air Act of 1967, the smelter was retrofitted to meet the new standards.

Hurley is a company town of neat houses and wide boulevards in the shadow of the smelter's smokestack. Although Phelps Dodge bought Kennecott Copper Corporation in 1986, the stack still reads "Kennecott" in vertical letters. Carrasco Avenue honors the area's first miner, and the depot, now the headquarters of the Southwestern Railroad, still surveys the tracks from the end of Cortez Street.

Bayard:
Branch-Line Standard Plans

The Pinos Altos range was the land of the Warm Springs Apaches, but after the Civil War, Anglo miners and gold prospectors began to occupy the hills to make their fortunes; the Apaches fought the foreign invaders. In 1866, the United States built Fort Bayard, named for Civil War brigadier general George Bayard, to protect the new settlers. The post was still active when the Silver City & Northern Railroad, a subsidiary of the Santa Fe, constructed a branch to reach area copper mines in 1892. The railroad established a new town south of the fort; originally named Hall's, it was changed to Bayard to honor the fort on April 12, 1899. Fort Bayard became an army hospital the next year.

In 1915, the Santa Fe built a village railroad station on Central Avenue at the end of Coffey Street west of the tracks. The Bayard depot is a "Frame Depot No. 2 for Branch Lines" from the railroad's "1910 Standards," with a significant modification: a

Fig. 72. Bayard depot, ca. 1996. Photo by author.

Fig. 73. Bayard depot, ca. 1996. Photo by author.

16-foot-long open-air waiting room on the north end. The open-air waiting room concept was common in the Santa Fe's masonry depots of the same era but rare in a frame depot. Another departure was the clapboard siding, made of 6-inch boards that were scored and shaped to look like a 3-inch lap, rather than the usual vertical board and batten. Other features of the depot—the gable roof, single-sided hexagonal bay window, and men's and women's waiting rooms on either side of the agent's bay—are typical of the standard.

There have been only minor changes to the Bayard depot. The open waiting room has been enclosed, a freight extension was added in 1922, and Santa Fe's colonial yellow paint scheme has been coated white. The building was retired in 1968 and purchased for $2,000 in 1974. Because the depot was used for storage, with windows and doors boarded up to deter vandals and theft, the interior is untouched, with many original features intact. The freight room includes the customary station agent signatures—such as "WE Bonnell—1923"—and the original freight-room doors with their glass panes and ornate brackets. In the interior of the public areas, original floors, wood windows, five-panel doors, and ticket window remain; the board-and-bead walls are painted a creamy yellow. Freight trains still pass by the Bayard depot, disappearing into the rolling Pinos Altos foothills.

CHAPTER FOURTEEN

Denver & Rio Grande System

In 1870, William Jackson Palmer, a Civil War brigadier general, founded the Denver & Rio Grande Railway in Colorado. Palmer, originally from Philadelphia, received his early training on the Pennsylvania Railroad before becoming the managing director of the Kansas Pacific after the war. In contrast to the more common transcontinental east-west routes, Palmer envisioned a north-south route through New Mexico and El Paso, linking Denver with Mexico City; he would also construct east-west feeders to encourage logging and mining in the sparsely inhabited Colorado territory.

The Rio Grande began building south from Denver in 1871, reaching Pueblo, Colorado, the next year. It was the first narrow-gauge railroad in the United States, with a track width of 3 feet; it imitated the even narrower (23.5 inches) Ffestiniog Railway in Wales to more easily negotiate the region's winding mountain passes. The Panic of 1873 halted construction on almost all U.S. railroads. When building began again, the Atchison, Topeka & Santa Fe built from the southeast, reaching Pueblo in 1876; it then built a standard-gauge line paralleling the Rio Grande's track to Denver. This ignited a fierce competition between the two companies that would last a decade.

Though the Denver & Rio Grande had already decided to build through Raton Pass, linking Colorado and New Mexico, the railroad spent time building branches to gold- and silver-mining towns instead of developing it; the Santa Fe initiated construction at the pass to claim the strategic location just before the Rio Grande dispatched its grading crews. The two railroads bitterly fought over other passes in Colorado, with legal battles reaching as high as the Supreme Court.

The long-standing argument was finally settled with a compromise reached in Boston in 1880. Called the Tripartite Agreement, or the Treaty of Boston, it limited the domains of each railroad company for ten years. The Santa Fe agreed to refrain from building in the Denver & Rio Grande's mountain preserve, and the Rio Grande agreed to limit construction to sixty miles south of its southernmost station of Conejos.

Palmer temporarily abandoned his plans for El Paso and built west to Salt Lake City. The railroad suffered financial losses, dividends to stockholders ceased, and the company went into receivership. Palmer eventually lost control of his railroad. With him, the dream of the Mexico City connection died, and the Denver & Rio Grande was transformed into an east-west line rather than the north-south line he had imagined.

Though the Rio Grande became primarily a Colorado/Utah railroad, it had several branches in New Mexico. The north-south Chile Line originally extended from Antonito, Colorado, to the southern point defined in the Treaty of Boston, the new town of Española, New Mexico. The remainder of the line to Santa Fe was constructed by another railroad company and purchased by the Rio Grande after the ten-year period. The San Juan Extension linked Alamosa, Colorado, with the silver-mining regions of Durango and Silverton. A branch off of this line was built in 1905 to reach Farmington, New Mexico, the center of a fruit-growing agricultural area. It was built in standard gauge to thwart the Southern Pacific, which also planned a line in the region. With the Southern Pacific threat gone, the tracks were converted to narrow gauge in 1923. Though several structures remain from the Rio Grande's lines in New Mexico, the only remaining structure on the Farmington Branch is the Aztec depot, now a private residence.

San Juan Extension: Narrow Gauge

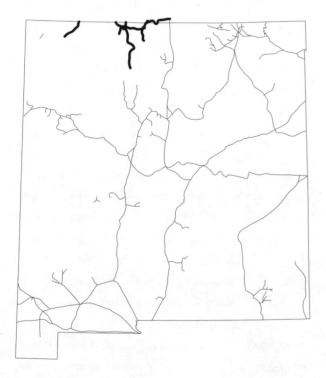

The 1880 Treaty of Boston settled the Denver & Rio Grande's disputes with rival Santa Fe Railway but restricted the Rio Grande's southern expansion. As a result, the railroad built west to exploit timber stands in northern New Mexico and mining districts in the San Juan Mountains. The San Juan Extension linked Antonito, on the Rio Grande's network in eastern Colorado, with silver mines in Durango and Silverton. The first portion to be

constructed, from Antonito to Chama, was the most difficult, negotiating the 10,015-foot Cumbres Pass and curves of twenty degrees. It featured two major bridges and, west of the pass, a 4 percent grade lasting fourteen miles. The line wove its way along the Colorado–New Mexico border, crossing it eleven times.

Chama, New Mexico, was designated a division point, and the Rio Grande constructed necessary locomotive maintenance and repair facilities. Service from eastern Colorado to Chama began in 1881; the railroad pressed on, reaching Durango in July and Silverton in 1882. In 1888, a spur was built from Chama to access timber stands to the south; this was extended to Tierra Amarilla in 1896.

Although the Antonito to Durango and Silverton line was built primarily for freight, its scenic route became popular with passengers. Regular passenger service was terminated in 1951, but excursion specials continued. In 1967, the Denver & Rio Grande abandoned the narrow-gauge line from Antonito to Durango, including a branch built to Farmington in 1905. The states of New Mexico and Colorado worked together to save the Antonito to Chama portion of the line, jointly purchasing the route and establishing the Cumbres & Toltec Scenic Railroad, a nonprofit excursion train, in 1970. Its first journey was on June 26, 1971. The sixty-four-mile railroad is a living museum dedicated to narrow gauge and the steam locomotive, with a working railyard and historic rolling stock.

Chama:
A Working Railyard from the Era of Steam
In the 1870s, Chama Crossing was a small Spanish sheep- and cattle-ranching settlement, named for its river location. The origin of the name Chama is lost; it may be

Fig. 74. Chama depot, ca. 2001. Photo by author.

the Spanish approximation of the Tewa name Tsama, meaning "here they wrestled," or of the word tzama, meaning red, the color of the river's water. The town of Chama, a lively, often lawless town of a thousand residents, was established by the Denver & Rio Grande in 1880 as a division point for its San Juan Extension. Shootings and holdups, typical of railroad towns, were common. The rowdy element was eventually reined in, and the town became a respectable community.

The railyard at Chama is still functional, serving an excursion railroad that runs on a sixty-four-mile section of San Juan Extension track. The railyard operates as it did in the steam era, with necessary buildings and structures, a railroad depot, wyes and sidings, stock-loading pens (at the south end of the yard, built in 1888), and a complement of rolling stock and machinery.

The primary purpose of a division point is the maintenance and repair of steam locomotives. The brick roundhouse and attached machine shop, where tools and supplies were stored, were built in 1899. Locomotive repairs occurred in the sheltered, nine-stall roundhouse (only two stalls remain). Engines were turned to access each stall with a turntable, later

removed and replaced with a wye south of the railyard; the triangular track configuration allowed a locomotive to make a three-point turn. Near the machine shop is the oil house, built in 1903 to provide storage for the assortment of oils and lubricants required by trains. An ash pit provided a place to clean the locomotive's firebox—carried out every four to six hours to rid it of the lumps of coal that did not burn completely.

On the west side of the tracks is a log bunkhouse, built in the 1880s and similar to the one in Sublette. It housed railroad crews and workers.

Movement of passengers and freight was another important railyard activity. The railroad depot was built in 1899 to replace a similar building destroyed by fire. Though still made of wood frame rather than more permanent masonry, it is one of the most ornate of the Rio Grande depots, befitting its division-point status. In addition to a clapboard base, board and batten siding, and fish-scale shingles in the gable, it features cross-gable pitches to highlight the east-facing agent's bay with ornamental gable brackets and decorative brick chimneys. The freight end to the south still contains the customary station agent signatures and now houses indoor restrooms, originally provided in outhouses. Inside, the building has its original wood trim and ticket window. The brick flue between the waiting room and agent's bay once served stoves in each room. To the south of the depot, a track scale built in 1929 once weighed loaded cars to determine the rate charged for freight shipments.

The railyard also contains structures that supply locomotives with water, coal, and sand for their westward runs. Water, needed for steam, was supplied via a pump from the Rio Chama to a wood tank built in 1897. Water tanks were needed every ten to twenty miles along the line; the Rio Grande's standard was 22

Fig. 75. Chama yard coal tipple, ca. 2001. Photo by author.

Fig. 76. Sublette section house and bunkhouse , ca. 1996. Photo by author.

feet in diameter and 15 feet tall. The tank at the rail-yard was a unique double-spouted design located between two tracks that could fill two locomotive tanks at once. It also stored water for use in the shops.

The sand house stored dried sand that engineers spread on the rails in steep grades or wet weather to prevent slippage. Next to the sand house is a coal tipple, built in 1924 to transfer coal to locomotives. The coal came from gondola cars that dropped their load into a drive-over car-dump hopper. Buckets on the east side of the tipple then lifted the coal over 50 feet to fill the elevated, seventy-five-ton coal bin. A mechanical building at the base of the tipple houses an oil-burning engine that provides the power to hoist the buckets; a pulley mechan-

ic's house is perched on top of the structure. The bin has sides of 3-inch wood planks and an outer framework of wood columns to keep the heavy load inside. The sloping floor of the bin helps the coal roll to the chute, which is inserted into a locomotive's tenders for filling.

Sublette:
Housing Railroad Crews

Sublette was established in 1881 as a locomotive siding and water stop, with a nearby stream supplying the water. The water tank was a wood-stave type; wood-stave construction consists of uniform strips of wood precision joined for strength. The tank was torn down in 1939 and replaced with a standpipe and underground concrete reservoir with a thirty-four-thousand-gallon capacity. The stop also includes a section house and two bunkhouses for railroad crews. One of the bunkhouses is a small wood-frame building built in the 1880s, with shingled siding and a railroad-tie foundation. It was originally used as a depot.

Lava Pump House: Quenching
a Locomotive's Never-Ending Thirst

The Denver & Rio Grande had several water stops along

Fig. 77. Lava pump house, ca. 1996. Photo by author.

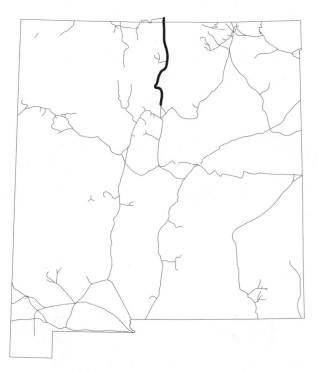

its line to satisfy thirsty locomotives' need for water to make steam. In 1883, water rights were conveyed to the railroad from Los Pinos Creek. The same year, the Rio Grande built a wood-frame pump house and dwelling for the pumper next to the creek at Lava, as well as a wood-stave tank adjacent to the tracks on the mesa top above. The pump house was replaced in the 1890s with a 28-foot by 32-foot gable-roofed building constructed of local lava rock. A cast-iron pipe drew water from the creek; the pump house included a brick-set locomotive boiler, Worthington pump, and No. 9 Cameron pump, to pump the water up to the tank. In the early 1900s, the railroad used twelve thousand gallons each day. A new water tank replaced the older tank in 1918, and the pumper's residence was removed in the 1930s, but the stone pump house remains. Its wood roof is deteriorating, and the creek threatens the small rock structure on its banks.

The Chile Line

The Treaty of Boston resolved the conflict between the Denver & Rio Grande and rival Atchison, Topeka & Santa Fe but also limited the Rio Grande's construction to a latitude sixty miles south of the railroad's south-

ernmost station in Conejos. In 1880 and 1881, it built a line from Antonito, Colorado, to this southern limit and established a town at the end of the tracks called Española. The Pullman fare from Denver to Española was $32.50, and the sleeping cars were named Aztec, La Senorita, San Ildefonso, and Tierra Amarilla.

Española, however, was still thirty-five miles from Santa Fe. The remainder of the trip was by stage-coach, and by the terms of the treaty, it would be ten years before the Rio Grande could extend the line. Several Santa Fe businessmen decided to build the railroad link themselves and formed the Texas, Santa Fe & Northern Railroad Company at the end of 1880. The first board of directors included many prominent Santa Fe residents, including Bernard Seligman and Zadoc Staab, but they had difficulty raising money. In 1882, the county voted in favor of bonds to help build the railroad, but financial troubles continued. Still lacking funds in 1886, Seligman found a New York syndicate interested in financing construction. Ohioan "General" Luther Meily headed the syndicate, and he became president of the Texas, Santa Fe & Northern.

Ironically, the link with the Denver & Rio Grande was built with materials from their rival, the Santa Fe, which underbid them on rail-shipment rates. Consequently, the railroad was constructed northward from Santa Fe rather than from Española. On November 6, 1886, the first locomotive ran on a short segment of track from the depot to the Arroyo de las Mascaras near Catron Avenue; after the long wait, the city was elated. The last spike was finally driven by Meily in Española on January 8, 1887, to connect the Texas, Santa Fe & Northern with the Rio Grande, and the next morning the first passenger train left Santa Fe. The railroad was called the Chile Line for the *chile ristras*, strings of red New Mexico peppers, that decorated the portales of the adobe houses along the route.

Santa Fe in the 1880s had dirt streets and a picket fence surrounding the plaza. The St. Francis Cathedral was under construction, and tracks to Española were in the middle of Guadalupe Street. A wye turned around locomotives returning north, with an engine house at the end of the wye.

Until the terms of the Treaty of Boston expired, the Rio Grande built above the southern limit in New Mexico, tapping into timber stands along the route, including short spurs to logging enterprises west of Tres Piedras, abandoned in 1892. Finally, in the early 1890s, the railroad began operating into Santa Fe, and passengers no longer changed trains in Española. The first through-service on the Chile Line was in 1893. The same year Meily decided to build from Santa Fe to Cerrillos and reorganized the line from Santa Fe to Española

under the new name Santa Fe Southern Railway. The trains and equipment were relettered but no construction began, and in 1895 the Denver & Rio Grande finally gained control of the lower portion of the Chile Line, calling it Rio Grande & Santa Fe Railroad Company until it consolidated its holdings in 1908.

Though Taos had always been the objective of many railroad proposals, the routes were never practical. The closest stop was twenty miles west at the Chile Line stop of Caliente (changed to Taos Junction after 1915). This was also the origination of the Halleck and Howard Lumber Company branches in 1914; logging was discontinued in 1927, and the tracks were removed in 1932.

The Chile Line suffered from declining revenues in the 1930s, went bankrupt, and received permission to abandon the line in 1941. The last train to Santa Fe was on August 30, 1941, and the *Albuquerque Tribune* ran a melancholy story: "The Denver and Rio Grande Railroad's last passenger train out of Santa Fe puffed off today for Antonito, Colorado leaving this capital city of New Mexico without regular rail connections for the first time in 60 years. . . . on it were a dozen passengers . . . including several who went along just to say goodbye to the train."[1] The Rio Grande began scrapping the rails one week later.

Embudo:
Garden of Rocks

When station agent Henry Wallace arrived in Embudo in 1912, the depot was a simple frame structure with clapboard siding, a deep roof overhang, simple brackets, and a separate freight house. It was one of the Rio Grande's first three stations in New Mexico, a coal and water stop built in 1880 and named Embudo, Spanish for "funnel," for its location

Fig. 78. Embudo depot, ca. 1919. Photo by William H. Roberts, courtesy of the Museum of New Mexico, neg. no. 149846.

Fig. 79. Embudo depot, 2003. Photo by author.

in the narrow river gorge.

Wallace was transferred to Embudo, a quiet stop on the line, because he was suffering from tuberculosis, but his health improved in northern New Mexico's favorable climate. He began applying a veneer of unbroken river stones to the depot, adding a cornice of broken mineralized quartz. He later covered the freight depot and his own house and began transforming the depot's interior. The waiting room had a quartz wainscot, concrete tabletops adorned with bridge spikes, and a ticket window of locomotive fire door chains anchored in a section of rail. He then built other structures on site for his family, including a cooking room lined with quartz and a summer sleeping room with a fireplace and canvas roof. A station sign of obsidian with quartz lettering, weighing six hundred pounds, once hung on a chain to greet the Rio Grande's trains.

Wallace thought he could finish his project and move on before it was discovered but was pleased when railroad officials and employees praised his undertaking. The Denver & Rio Grande sent carloads of rock and cement so that he could continue. Embudo was a meal stop in the 1920s, and passengers who saw the inimitable world he had built sent more stones and rocks from their homes around the country. In a July 1926 article, the Denver & Rio Grande's magazine gushed over his "unique and rare work," which they termed a "Garden of Rocks."[2]

Wallace was Embudo's last station agent, remaining until the stop closed in 1934. He was transferred to Santa Fe and died the following year. The ruins of his remarkable endeavor remain on site, though there have been changes since the 1930s. A stone-covered structure, used as a dining room, was added to the northeast end of the depot when the site was a boys' camp. This and the depot are now a private residence adjacent to a riverside restaurant. There is still evidence of the depot's origins as a frame railroad station, including the Rio Grande's triangular wooden brackets, a gabled roof with a deep overhang of wood boards, and the windows and doors, inset in stonework, with their familiar proportions. Behind the depot are the reminders that Embudo is there as a result of the trains: the old railroad grade, the collapsing freight room, and the typical wood-stave water tower with its conical top.

CHAPTER FIFTEEN

Colorado & Southern and the Colmor Cutoff

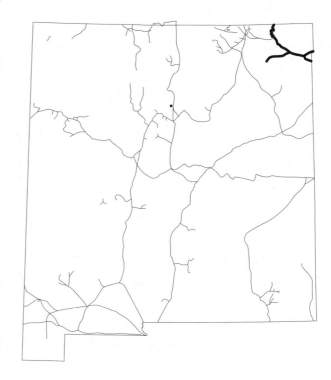

With the goal of linking Denver to Fort Worth, Texas, by rail, two railroad entrepreneurs agreed to pool their resources and each build a portion of the line. Coloradoan John Evans began building south from Denver in 1881 with two railroad companies: the Denver, Texas & Gulf and Denver, Texas & Fort Worth. Texan Grenville Dodge, formerly chief engineer in charge of building the Texas & Pacific Railway, built northwest from Fort Worth under the name Fort Worth & Denver City Railway. On March 14, 1888, the railroads met near the construction camp of Folsom, New Mexico, at a location christened Union Park.

Each line built its own stations. In New Mexico, the Denver, Texas & Fort Worth had a depot in Folsom, and the Fort Worth & Denver City had depots in Des Moines, Clayton, Grenville, and Mt. Dora with shingled hipped roofs, light-colored wood siding, rectangular agent's bays, and dark green trim.

With their connection from Denver to Fort Worth in place, Evans and Dodge began building logging branch lines. Managers of the Maxwell Land Grant persuaded them to build the Catskill and Vasquez branches from Colorado into New Mexico to access their timber stands; they were completed in 1890. The

nine-mile Dunn's and Newton Branch was built from Catskill and Vasquez between 1890 and 1897.

With financial difficulties at the sawmills and the main line, the Colorado & Southern Railway acquired the lines in 1898. Though there were already Denver, Texas & Fort Worth and Fort Worth & Denver City stations on the line, and the train stopped for passengers, there was no official passenger service. The sawmills remained unsuccessful, and New Mexico's logging branches were abandoned in 1902. By 1908, when the Colorado & Southern was purchased by the Burlington Northern, only five miles of branch track remained in Colorado; by 1940, this too was abandoned.

The Colorado & Southern line experienced terrible snowstorms that trapped trains for two weeks, and train robberies, including Black Jack Ketchum's last holdup, two miles north of Des Moines (for which he was tried and hanged in nearby Clayton in 1901). But the line is still active, hauling freight from Texas to Colorado. The only railroad depots remaining are the Denver Texas & Fort Worth's 1888 two-story wood-frame station in Folsom, and the Fort Worth & Denver City's station in Grenville, both residences.

In 1931, the Santa Fe built the Colmor Cutoff from Oklahoma to Farley, with an agreement to use Colorado & Southern tracks from Clayton to Mt. Dora. The cutoff was intended to join the Santa Fe's main line at Colmor, eleven miles south of Springer, but work on the remaining thirty-five miles was deferred during the Great Depression. Even with a more favorable economy, the line was not completed; it was often called the "line to nowhere." Two Colmor Cutoff depots remain in New Mexico: the Des Moines depot, relocated by the Santa Fe from Raton, and the Clayton depot, built in 1931 in the same Tudor Revival style as its Cimarron, Kansas depot. Like the Colorado & Southern depots, these stations are also residences.

CHAPTER SIXTEEN

Southern Pacific System

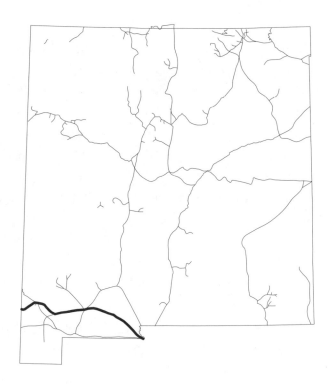

The Southern Pacific Railroad was originally chartered to link San Francisco with El Paso, Texas. The Central Pacific acquired the Southern Pacific in 1868; it was the most powerful railroad company in the western United States at the time, with a monopoly over Southern California traffic. The Central Pacific's "Big Four"—Leland Stanford, Charles Crocker, Collis Huntington, and Mark Hopkins—revised the Southern Pacific's mission, extending its terminus to New Orleans to provide a valuable California–Gulf of Mexico connection.

Subsidiary Southern Pacific Railroad Company of New Mexico was incorporated in 1879 to build through Lordsburg and Deming. This main line was the only track built by the Southern Pacific in the state. The remaining Southern Pacific lines were absorbed into the Southern Pacific's system when it acquired the El Paso & Southwestern lines in 1924. The El Paso & Southwestern lines included the El Paso & Northeastern system, purchased in 1905. In 1975, the Southern Pacific took over the Chicago, Rock Island & El Paso extension of the main El Paso & Northeastern line, from Santa Rosa to Dalhart, Texas.

Southern Pacific Main Line

On February 2, 1848, the United States and Mexico signed the Treaty of Guadalupe Hidalgo. The treaty ended the Mexican-American War but created a dispute over the location of the northern border of Mexico. The Gasden Purchase of 1853 negotiated by James Gasden, a railroad executive from North Carolina sent by President Franklin, finally settled that dispute. The United States, which wanted the northern Mexico territory for a southern railroad and mail route, paid financially strapped Mexico $10 million for portions of Arizona and New Mexico. The U.S. government commissioned surveys for transcontinental railroad routes that same year.

Four years later, the Butterfield Overland Mail stagecoach first ran through Gasden Purchase territory from Tipton, Missouri, to San Francisco. The stagecoach rate was 10¢ per letter. Passengers paid $200 each way or 15¢ a mile to ride on comfortable

Concord stages and, when needed, more rugged Celerity stages. The survey of the Southern Pacific's main line to link California with Louisiana and the Gulf of Mexico followed the western portion of the Butterfield Overland stage. The railroad built east from San Diego, through Lordsburg, reaching Deming in late 1880. The Atchison, Topeka & Santa Fe tracks arrived almost three months later, in early March, linking the two railroads and completing the second U.S. transcontinental railroad. The Southern Pacific continued east, completing the line to El Paso on May 19, 1881, now twenty-three days ahead of the Santa Fe, which built south from Rincon.

Fig. 80. Deming depot, 2001. Photo by author.

Most of the traffic on the Southern Pacific's line was from interstate shipping, with minor traffic from local mines and livestock centers. Despite minimal passenger traffic, Southern Pacific depots, with their hipped moss-green roofs, golden yellow paint with a darker wainscot, brown trim, and white window sashes, were a common sight in southwestern New Mexico. The only remaining depots built by the railroad are in Deming and Columbus.

Deming:
A Depot in Two Time Zones

The original settlement near present-day Deming was called New Chicago, a tent city officially named on October 15, 1881. New Chicago was abandoned when Southern Pacific surveyors platted a new townsite to the west; despite the warnings of locals, they found abundant water. The new town was named by Southern Pacific Railroad official and Big Four member Charles Crocker to honor his wife, Mary Ann Deming, daughter of an Indiana sawmill owner.

Southern Pacific tracks arrived in Deming on December 15, 1880, designated a division point, and

then continued eastward. The Santa Fe Railways tracks reached Deming on March 8, 1881, and the two railroads were linked with a commemorative silver spike. At the junction, the Southern Pacific constructed a large 39- by 325-foot frame station north of their main line and south of the Santa Fe's tracks. The building, completed in 1881, was shared by the Santa Fe, which occupied the east end and had a clock on Mountain Railway time; the Southern Pacific used the west end with a clock with Southern Pacific time. Between these one-story ends was a two-story central portion that served as a hotel and lunchroom, with rooms for $6 and meals for $1 extra. A porch with western-style columns encircled the first story, and the hotel had a second-story balcony. The hipped roof, a Southern Pacific trademark, had several ornate brick chimneys.

The Southern Pacific's west end included a railroad office, telegraph office, Adams Express Company office, Wells Fargo office, and waiting rooms. In addition to the hotel and lunchroom, there were roundhouses for both railroads and a coal tower to the east. Beginning in 1882, the line provided a railway post office (RPO), which started from Deming and ran through Arizona to Los Angeles and on to San Francisco. At 1,198 miles, the RPO was the longest on record; it operated seven days a week and was a vast improvement over the mail stages, which took twenty-five days from Missouri to San Francisco.

Deming also had a newspaper, started by J. E. Curren, who established several papers; he named it the *Deming Headlight*, after the headlight of a Southern Pacific engine. The newspaper mocked the developing town, quoting a visitor, who quipped: "Deming morals are not to be discussed in a newspaper until she has some."[1]

Of Deming's many railroad buildings, only the station remains, and it was drastically altered in 1930 when the removal of the second story eliminated the hotel. The east and west ends were demolished, reducing the building to 113 feet long. A new hipped roof with simple two-part brackets was added. Within the jumble of doors, windows, and trim are reminders of its elegant past, including typical narrow double-hung windows, freight-room doors with divided transoms, and horizontal siding painted Southern Pacific yellow. A large, ornate brick chimney on the west end remains from the original hotel. Inside is the agent's ticket window with a starflake glass pattern.

El Paso & Northeastern System: Connections, Coal, Timber, and Tourists

Cattle rancher Charles B. Eddy's first railroad venture was the Pecos Valley Railroad with J. J. Hagerman, built to settle the Pecos Valley and ship its agricultural products to Texas and beyond. After the railroad's continued financial troubles, Eddy pulled out of the partnership and retreated to El Paso in 1895. He was soon planning a new railroad, one to link El Paso with

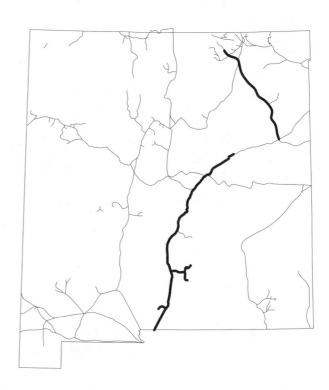

Chicago. The *Santa Fe New Mexican* ran a front-page story on October 21, 1897, with a headline that was more like an advertisement. "C. B. Eddy's Sagacity, Pluck and Perseverance Carry the Day—Organization of a Company to Build 150 Miles of Railroad in New Mexico; Money on Hand for its Completion; Extensive Coal Fields, Magnificent Agricultural Lands, Vast Mineral Regions & Fine Lands Reached by New Line; Trains to Run in 12 Months; First Sure Harbinger of Prosperity and Development After a Long Depression in Sunny New Mexico."[2]

The El Paso press initially called Eddy's new road the White Oaks Railroad, for the booming gold-mining town that it would eventually bypass, but the name El Paso & Northeastern was adopted in 1897. Construction began later that year from El Paso toward the Oliver Lee Ranch, which Eddy purchased and subdivided to create a new town for the railroad's headquarters and repair shops. The town was named Alamogordo, Spanish for "fat poplar," referring to the cottonwood trees that grow near water sources. In 1898, Eddy sold lots in Alamogordo, and the first locomotive came from El Paso. The following year, the line was extended north toward Carrizozo.

Meanwhile, the Chicago, Rock Island & El Paso, a subsidiary of the Chicago, Rock Island & Pacific, planned to connect with the El Paso & Northeastern system at Santa Rosa. Eddy formed the El Paso & Rock Island Railway Company to build the portion of his line from Carrizozo to Santa Rosa in 1902. The two lines met as planned, and the "Arrow Route," linking El Paso and Chicago, began operating on February 1.

Since railroads require timber and coal to operate, Eddy built branches from the main line east into the coalfields in Coalora and the forests of the Sacramento Mountains, beginning around 1898.

The Coalora line was extended in 1900 to Capitan, but as these coalfields were limited, Eddy explored other sources including White Oaks, which also proved disappointing. He eventually secured an option on coal under John Dawson's Ranch in northern New Mexico. With permission to use the Rock Island line from Santa Rosa to Tucumcari, Eddy began constructing a branch to connect Dawson and Tucumcari in 1902. Operations began on the Dawson Railway in 1903. The line was eventually dismantled, but the former grade from Dawson to French, on the Santa Fe Railway's main line, was used again in 1965, when the Santa Fe built a branch to York Canyon, a few miles beyond Dawson, for Kaiser Steel. When the mill closed in 1983, the line was dismantled again.

Large quantities of timber were necessary in railroad construction for the many crossties, trestles, depots, coal towers, and buildings required. The El Paso & Northeastern's logging railroad was constructed by subsidiary Alamogordo & Sacramento Mountain Railway beginning in 1898 from the main line near Alamogordo, reaching Toboggan in 1899. Engineer Horace Sumner laid out the mountainous route in standard gauge, a feat of engineering. With an elevation gain of 4,700 feet in only thirty-two miles, the "Cloud-Climbing Railroad" had 5.2 percent grades and 330 curves. Some of these curves were as sharp as thirty degrees and could not be traversed by standard locomotives, so engines were altered in division shops in El Paso. At the turn of the century, the Cloud-Climbing Railroad was the highest standard-gauge line in the country. Although narrow gauge, which had cars with a smaller turning radius, was generally reserved for mountain railroads, the use of standard gauge eliminated expensive car-to-car transfer of shipments to the main El Paso & Northeastern line. Eddy extended the Cloud-Climbing Railroad numerous times over several years. When it reached Cloudcroft in 1900, he built a passenger depot and resort to attract Texan tourists to the dramatic setting. By 1938, the line carried only freight; it was abandoned in 1947, and the railroad depot was removed two years later.

In 1905, Phelps Dodge, in need of new coal sources, purchased the El Paso & Northeastern lines and absorbed them into its El Paso & Southwestern system. When Phelps Dodge decided to concentrate on its copper business, the Southern Pacific bought its railroads in 1924. The Southern Pacific took over the Rock Island segment in 1975 and continues to operate the main line.

There were once several depots and maintenance facilities on the route, including shops at Alamogordo and Carrizozo. The Ancho depot is now a private museum, and the Corona depot, relocated to Alamogordo, is a model-railroad museum. The Duran depot, built around 1902, is typical of the railroad's depots, but is now a residence in Santa Rosa. There are still some remnants of the dramatic Cloud-Climbing Railroad, including the hotel and remains of the wooden trestles that negotiated the narrow canyons of the Sacramento Mountains.

Corona:
Freight Room at Track Height

The railroad depot originally built by the El Paso & Northeastern to serve Torrance in 1899 has moved several times, with two locations during its service to the railroad and more afterward. Like most wood-frame depots, it was designed to be placed on railroad flatcars and relocated as needed. Like its larger counterpart in Ancho, it has a hipped roof, double-hung windows, horizontal lapped siding with a vertical base, and a raised rectangular agent's bay. Unlike Ancho, the depot's baggage room was at track height rather than railcar height, and therefore it had no freight platform.

After Torrance, the station served Corona, a sparsely settled area that grew as a result of railroad traffic. The name Corona was chosen by the El Paso & Northeastern, but the reason for the railroad's choice is unclear. Spanish for "crown," Corona may have been inspired by a small peak nearby or may have been selected because the station was at the high point of the line, at 6,724 feet. The town, on the east side of the tracks, moved to the west when U.S. Highway 54 was laid out in the 1920s. It continued to thrive as an agricultural and trade center but withered in the 1940s.

The Southern Pacific took over the El Paso & Northeastern's lines and structures in 1924. When the Southern Pacific retired Corona's depot, it was relo-

Fig. 81. Corona depot, 1995. Photo by author.

cated again in 1974 to Alamogordo; it now houses a model-railroad museum on the city's main thoroughfare. It has suffered many changes, including a non-historic paint scheme over the Southern Pacific's golden yellow with brown trim. The freight door has been removed and replaced with a window. A large rear addition and a shed with barn-style doors blur the plan of what was once a compact building with a baggage room, agent's bay, and single waiting room.

Cloudcroft:
The Cloud-Climbing Railroad

The El Paso & Northeastern's Alamogordo & Sacramento Railway, known as the Cloud-Climbing Railroad for its winding path into the Sacramento Mountains, was created to access plentiful timber. The cool mountain air and forested setting inspired railroad owner Charles Eddy to establish a resort in the hills. The first building to be constructed was the Pavilion, built in 1899. During construction of the line, Pavilion guests rode in horse-drawn carriages from Toboggan to Cloudcroft. When the railroad was complete, the town

Fig. 82. Mexican Trestle,
Alamogordo & Sacramento
Railway, 2001. Photo by
Jud Cervenak.

was reached only by train, a journey of two hours and twenty minutes over twenty-six miles of hairpin turns. Eddy advertised Cloudcroft in his home base of El Paso, and many Texan tourists escaped the intense summer heat in the mountain resort.

The railroad traversed twenty-seven bridges, including the Mexican Trestle, completed in November 1899. The curving trestle is 323 feet long and sits 52 feet above the canyon floor. It consists of 12-inch-square timbers spaced 15 feet apart, with the rails and crossties placed on 8- by 16-inch stringers. The structure is held together with cast-iron spacers and ¾-inch bolts. A layer of gravel was used to protect the ties and stringers from sparks. When the train reached the trestle, a whistle sounded that could be heard at the depot, announcing that the train would arrive in fifteen minutes. Passengers traveled in open-air cars that were built on boxcar frames to provide sweeping vistas of the thrilling ride.

Cloudcroft was immediately successful as a resort. Construction on the first Lodge began in spring 1900. It was complete by June the following year but was consumed by fire only eight years later, on June 13, 1909. Construction on a new hotel on a dramatic hill-top site began the following April, and the building was completed in 1911. A square tower with a fanciful domed cupola marks the entry. The front verandah is now enclosed but was once an airy place to relax. The Pavilion also burned, in both 1919 and 1922, but was rebuilt in 1923. When the El Paso & Southwestern took over the El Paso & Northeastern lines in 1905, they also took over operations at the Lodge, and in the 1930s famous New Mexico hotelier Conrad Hilton managed the hotel.

Gradually, tourists favored automobiles over trains, and the last passenger excursion on the Cloud-Climbing Railroad was in February 1938. Timber continued to be hauled on the line until September 12,

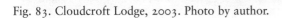

Fig. 83. Cloudcroft Lodge, 2003. Photo by author.

Fig. 84. Ancho depot, 2001. Photo by author.

1947. Only two days later, the Southern Pacific, which acquired all of the El Paso & Southwestern's lines in 1924, began pulling track, ties, and spikes to sell for scrap. It left behind the old railroad beds and wooden trestles spanning the canyons, which then deteriorated and fell into piles of wood on the canyon floors. The Mexican Trestle has been restored, the Pavilion is now a bed-and-breakfast, and the Lodge is still an elegant destination resort.

Ancho:

The Brick Boom

Ancho was founded in 1899 as a stop on the El Paso & Northeastern's main line, a shipping supply point for local ranchers. Spanish for "wide," the name reflects its spacious valley location. Two years after the railroad arrived, gypsum deposits were found in the nearby Jicarilla Mountains; plaster mills, gypsum-testing plants, and sawmills were constructed in Ancho and the town became famous for its plaster. The valley also yielded fire clay, and a plant was built to produce the golden bricks. Hundreds of tons were sent to San Francisco for rebuilding after the 1906 earthquake.

The wood-frame railroad depot was built in 1902.

It was typical of depots on the El Paso & Northeastern line, with a hipped roof and tall, rectangular agent's bay, which has the appearance of a tower. This look is enhanced by a band of windows on the tower under the eaves; these are blocked by the ceiling inside, and therefore are purely decorative. The window-sash pattern (four vertical panes over two), the board and batten base, and lapped wood siding are also typical features of depots on the line. The depot's woodstoves were served by two brick chimneys; one warmed the east-end waiting room and the other the agent's office. When the Southern Pacific took over the line in 1924, the depot was painted in standard Southern Pacific colors: green roof, yellow siding, and brown trim. Though the paint has now faded, the color scheme remains.

The depot also has its original telegraph and semaphore, used by the station agent to transmit train orders to passing trains. Dispatch sent a telegraphed message to the agent, who then wrote the orders on onionskin paper. He notified the train crew that there were orders by shifting the indicators on the semaphore and placed the onionskin paper in wire holders with bamboo hoops to hand to the engineer and conductor; they took the orders and cast off the hoops to be reused. Inside the depot is an original train-order hoop.

When Ancho's brick plant closed in 1921, residents moved away to find new jobs, and the town's population declined. In the 1950s, U.S. Highway 54 bypassed the town by two and a half miles; the school, built of Ancho brick in 1930, closed. In 1959, the depot was retired and relocated south of the tracks, housing the town post office and a museum called My House of Old Things. Though the museum is still open, the post office was closed in 1973, and mail is delivered from Carrizozo. The population in Ancho has declined, but in many ways it stays the same, with a railroad depot in a setting of juniper- and piñon-covered rolling hills, an old schoolhouse demonstrating the quality of the local brick, and the sounds of the trains as they roar past.

Capitan:
Satisfying the Railroad's Craving for Coal

The Mescalero Apache were hunter-gatherers who lived in the plains and made frequent trips into the Sacramento and Capitan mountain ranges to hunt antelope. They had little contact with the Spanish missionaries who sought to convert other tribes and did not experience conflict until Anglos settled in the region after New Mexico became a U.S. territory in 1850. The government established Fort Stanton in 1855 to protect these settlers from the Apaches, and communities began to develop around it. Seaborn T. Gray homesteaded nearby in 1884, opened a small store in 1887, and applied for a post office for the new town of Gray in 1894.

A few years later, in 1899, Charles Eddy's El Paso & Northeastern railroad built its line from El Paso to Carrizozo. Eddy purchased coalfields in Coalora and built a spur to access them the same year. By June,

Fig. 85. Capitan depot, 2001. Photo by Jud Cervenak.

however, coal production declined. Eddy bought coal-rich land from Gray in January 1900 through a subsidiary of his railroad, the Alamogordo Improvement Company, and extended the spur. On a portion of his new land, Eddy platted a town site across from Gray's homestead, absorbed the fledgling town, and renamed it Capitan for the mountains to the northeast. The first lot in Capitan was sold on March 4, 1900, and within a year the population had reached a thousand. Some of the new settlers came from Coalora, transporting entire houses.

Coalora's depot, built in 1900, was eventually relocated to Capitan as well, in 1936. The simplified El Paso & Northeastern depot has the typical hipped, shingled roof with a generous overhang, but without a projecting agent's bay. On its main-line depots, the railroad used lapped horizontal siding with board and batten bases, but board and batten covers the entire exterior of this branch-line depot. The details are also relatively plain: an unadorned wood cornice, straight brackets, and simple two pane over two pane double-hung windows rather than the more stylish vertical four pane over two seen in the Ancho and Corona depots. The plan was also simple: a waiting room on the east, an agent's office, a baggage room at street level, and a freight room at railcar level.

The train ran two times a week in the early years, but by the 1930s, it ran only on Fridays. For a long time, a letter could be mailed at the depot, where it was sorted in a railroad post office (RPO) car to be later distributed in El Paso. The letter was postmarked with the words "RPO Capitan/El Paso."

It was due to one highly successful and morally questionable local merchant, George Titsworth, that the railroad spur was active so long. Titsworth earned his cutthroat reputation by acting as creditor to new settlers and taking portions of their land when they couldn't pay. He was the main supplier to Fort Stanton, which became a hospital after 1896. Though the railroad wanted to close the Capitan spur, he needed the link to provide his supplies and convinced the El Paso & Northeastern to keep the line active. The tracks were finally dismantled in 1943, and Titsworth died six years later.

Capitan is now more famous as the birthplace of Smokey, a bear cub rescued from a forest fire in the Capitan Gap in 1950; he became the living embodiment of the Smokey Bear symbol of fire prevention featured on a National Forest Service poster designed six years earlier. The Smokey Bear State Park has owned Capitan's railroad depot since 1975 but uses it only for storage. From its strategic downtown location, the building still overlooks the old railroad grade to the north and awaits a revival.

Chicago, Rock Island & El Paso Railroad: The Golden State Route

The Chicago, Rock Island & Pacific was originally chartered as the Rock Island & La Salle Rail Road Company in Illinois in 1847. In 1892, the railroad

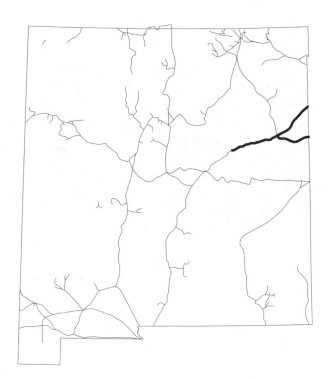

completed a line from Kansas through Oklahoma into Texas. They began developing their Kansas City line in late 1900 to connect the main line (from Liberal, Kansas) with El Paso, Texas.

The Rock Island negotiated with Charles Eddy of the El Paso & Northeastern, which already had a line from El Paso to Carrizozo, and it was determined that each line would build a portion of the remaining 391 miles, meeting at Santa Rosa. The Rock Island constructed its New Mexico portion under the subsidiary Chicago, Rock Island & El Paso in 1901 and early 1902. Considerable grading was required to traverse the rolling hills of eastern New Mexico, but the Rock Island reached Santa Rosa first and waited for Eddy to complete his tracks. On February 1, 1902, the last spike was driven to connect the two railroads. The route was called the Golden State Route, and the

Fig. 86. Tucumcari depot, ca. 2001. Photo by author.

Fig. 87. Tucumcari depot, ca. 2001. Photo by author.

Golden State Limited passenger train went into service in November, offering a winter train to California.

In 1910, the Rock Island, under the name Tucumcari & Memphis Railroad, completed a line from Amarillo to Glenrio (near the New Mexico border) and into New Mexico, connecting with the Golden State Route in Tucumcari. This created a route from Memphis to the Pacific coast via Oklahoma City and Amarillo, and year-round service was provided to California until 1968.

Though the Rock Island served fourteen states and had nearly eight thousand miles of main track, it was not a financial success. In 1975, the Rock Island's lines were acquired by other railroads; Southern Pacific subsidiary St. Louis Southwestern Railway took over both the Golden State and Tucumcari to Memphis routes.

Tucumcari:
Six Shooter Siding

Liberty, New Mexico, located north of Pajarito Creek in the shadow of Liberty Mesa, was a lively western town in the 1870s, founded for soldiers stationed at Fort Bascom during the Civil War. When the Rock Island Railroad laid tracks to the east in 1901, five businessmen from Liberty—M. B. Goldenberg, A. D. Goldenberg, Jacob Wertheim, J. A. Street, and Lee Smith—purchased land directly on the line. They donated 120 acres for a new townsite, formally named Douglas. The name Douglas was used until the first trains arrived in 1902; it was then changed to Tucumcari for the 5,000-foot mountain two miles south. Tucumcari may be a version of the Plains Indian word *tukamukaru*, meaning "to lie in wait for something to approach," since the mountain was a natural lookout.

The railroad established a division point, and, as Fort Bascom had already closed, half the population of Liberty moved to Tucumcari, spelling the end of the former settlement. Tucumcari's many tents and lack of permanent buildings earned it the nickname Ragtown. Alternatively it was called Six Shooter Siding for the saloons and gambling halls that attracted outlaws and gunfights.

Soon there were two westbound and two eastbound passenger trains, a mail train, an express, and at least one freight train each way through Tucumcari

Fig. 88. Tucumcari railyard, 1948. Courtesy of the Museum of New Mexico, neg. no. 99681.

daily. A railroad post office car postmarked mail with the Tucumcari/El Paso stamp and sent it to El Paso for distribution. When Quay County was formed in 1903, the community was still made of tents and lacked water. Water was hauled daily and delivered to each house, at the rate of 50¢ a barrel, but the residents stayed and eventually created a permanent settlement.

Tucumcari's depot was built by the Rock Island in 1926, with brick walls coated in stucco and wood trusses supporting the roof. The Mission Revival style features dramatically curved parapets, arched windows, a gable tile roof, and brick detailing. Quatrefoils, accented coping, shaped canales, and the lacy letters of the station sign demonstrate the Rock Island's facility with the style, which they did not use on other depots. On the south facade, facing Main Street, there is evidence of a now-infilled open breezeway.

The large depot and nearby roundhouse, which has since been demolished, also served the El Paso & Northeastern's 1903 line to French in Colfax County and the Rock Island's 1910 line from El Paso that connected to its Golden State Route in Tucumcari. The west end of the depot was a restaurant concession, operated as the twenty-four-hour Interstate by the Van Noy Interstate Company. It was later a Beanery Restaurant, the Southern Pacific's answer to the Santa Fe's Harvey Houses.

Passenger service ended in 1968, although the Southern Pacific, which took over the Golden State Route in 1975, still runs freight on the main line. The other lines to Tucumcari have been dismantled: the last train on the El Paso & Northeastern's route to French was in 1963, and the last train from Amarillo to Memphis was in 1980.

El Paso & Southwestern:
The Copper Queen's Bisbee Road

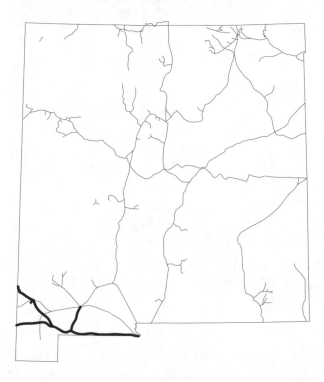

Fig. 89. Tyrone depot, ca. 1968. Courtesy of the Museum of New Mexico, neg. no. 44414.

The Southern Pacific and Santa Fe railroads joined in Deming in 1881, creating the second U.S. transcontinental railroad. The Southern Pacific then extended its line from Deming through El Paso, continuing to the Gulf of Mexico. Though the Southern Pacific dominated southwestern New Mexico, other railroads began building short branches.

In 1884, the Santa Fe, building under the name Arizona & New Mexico, constructed a line from Arizona to Lordsburg, a stop on the Southern Pacific, for Arizona Copper. The Copper Queen Mine, a subsidiary of Phelps Dodge, completed a thirty-six-mile route in 1889 to connect with the Arizona & New Mexico; the Bisbee, Arizona, mine sought to transport copper from its local smelter to an El Paso refinery. The line was extended to Benson

in 1894 to provide another freight connection, in this case with the Southern Pacific. When a larger smelter was constructed in the new town of Douglas, Arizona, named for Copper Queen owner Dr. James Douglas, the line was extended south. Ore was then taken by rail to the Douglas smelter before being transported back to the Southern Pacific line to be shipped to El Paso.

Douglas and Phelps Dodge soon became frustrated with the Southern Pacific, which often failed to keep up with freight demands, and formed the El Paso & Southwestern Railroad to bypass it. Construction began in 1900, simultaneously east from Douglas and south from the Santa Fe's track at Deming. The gap was closed in February 1902, and construction continued east from Hermanas through the border town of Columbus toward El Paso. The Southern Pacific tried to prevent the El Paso & Southwestern's parallel route by refusing to ship building materials and by obtaining a court order to stop the new railroad from using its desired route into Texas. Despite this interference, the Bisbee Road reached El Paso in November. It offered an easier grade than the Southern Pacific, and, according to the *History of New Mexico* from 1907, the "road is finely constructed, having all the appliances of modern railroads, and nowhere has the work or material been skimped or slighted."[3]

In 1902, Douglas convinced the management of the Arizona & New Mexico to extend its line from Lordsburg to Hachita. Phelps Dodge built other branches in Arizona, but only one more line in New Mexico, a spur from the Santa Fe's Silver City branch to access its Tyrone copper mine in 1914; it was built by subsidiary Burro Mountain Railroad. The town of Tyrone was built in 1915, designed by architect Bertram Goodhue (also in charge of the California International Exposition buildings built in San Diego the same year). He was chosen by Douglas's wife, who envisioned the new company town as a "dream city." The Mission Revival style included arched colonnades and elaborate buildings grouped around a central plaza. The depot/post office, which cost $100,000 to build, was an architectural masterpiece, with marble benches heated with hot-air pipes.

Now the El Paso & Southwestern dominated railroading in southwestern New Mexico and southeastern Arizona. As the demand for copper grew, Phelps Dodge built larger smelters. These operated on coal and coke, and so in 1905 the El Paso & Southwestern purchased the El Paso & Northeastern system, with lines into the rich coalfields of northern New Mexico. In January 1922, the railroad merged with the Arizona & New Mexico. Unfortunately, the price of copper plummeted after World War I, and copper mines, including Tyrone, closed. In an effort to focus on copper production, in 1924 Phelps Dodge sold its railroad network, now over twelve hundred miles, to the Southern Pacific for about $64 million.

The El Paso & Southwestern was gradually dismantled, beginning with the Hermanas to Deming portion in 1929. The main Bisbee Road remained and experienced a brief revival during World War II, when forty trains a day transported troops. In 1955, the Southern Pacific renamed the route the "Southline" to distinguish it from their "Northline" through Lordsburg and Deming. Only six years later, a Southern Pacific study showed that abandoning the line would save $600,000 a year. The last train ran on December 20, 1961, but the tracks and structures remained for another two years. Phelps Dodge, also in pursuit of increased profits, demolished Tyrone in 1967 to access deep copper deposits.

As the railroad employees moved, the farming and ranching communities along the line became ghost towns. The railroad grade, partial trestles, and bridges are still visible along New Mexico State Road 9. But of the many El Paso & Southwestern depots, with their hipped roofs and deep overhangs, only the Animas, Hachita, and Columbus depots remain. Animas and Hachita are in private hands, but the Columbus depot is a museum.

Columbus:
A Border Town

Columbus began as a border station across from Palomas in the Mexican state of Chihuahua around 1890. In 1902, the El Paso & Southwestern's line passed through on its way to copper refineries in El Paso, and the town moved three miles north to a

Fig. 90. Columbus depot, 2001. Photo by author.

location on the route; the border site soon faded. The same year, the railroad built a depot, pump house, and section house, and across the street a frame, hipped roof customs house was built to regulate trade from Palomas.

The railroad depot was also of frame construction, with second-story stationmaster living quarters accessed by a steep stairway. It had the El Paso & Southwestern's typical hipped roof but without the usual deep overhang. A one-story portion on the east end stored freight. Both sections had horizontal siding with a base of vertical wood boards.

Though Columbus was on the route of other proposed railroads, including a line that would link the town to Palomas and another that would pass through on its way from northern Mexico to Salt Lake City, plans never materialized. The roadbed of the Columbus-Palomas line later served as a highway between the two towns.

In late 1914 and early 1915, the United States became concerned that Pancho Villa and his army of Villistas were planning to enter the United States. Camp Furlong, headquarters of the Thirteenth U.S. Cavalry, was established in Columbus to prevent Villa from crossing the border. However, before dawn on March 9, 1916, about five hundred Villistas on horseback surprised the town; the raid lasted three hours before Villa's men retreated to Mexico. Most casualties were Villistas but also included U.S. soldiers and civilians. The attack was the last foreign invasion of the continental United States. A week later, the "Punitive Expedition" of cavalry soldiers, led by General John Pershing, left Camp Furlong and entered Mexico to search for Pancho Villa. Both soldiers and supplies arrived in Columbus by railroad, stopping at the depot before entering the army camp. The expedition became a training ground for World War I; it was the last time a horse cavalry was used in a large military operation and the first time cars, motorcycles, trucks, and armored vehicles were used. The population of Columbus grew to ten thousand people before dropping dramatically when the Punitive Expedition, which never found Pancho Villa, was discontinued eleven months later. He was assassinated in 1923.

The Southern Pacific, which purchased the El Paso & Southwestern system in 1924, abandoned the railroad depot in 1959 and donated it to Columbus; the last run of the Sunset Limited was on December 19, 1961. The railroad removed the tracks two years later, and residents continued to use the roadbed for trips to El Paso.

There are many historic buildings in Columbus, from both the railroad era and the Pancho Villa raid. Several buildings remain from Camp Furlong, including a headquarters building, a recreation hall, and a tiny adobe army court and jail. The Hoover Hotel, the site of heavy fighting during the raid; the elementary school where women and children hid; and the Rodriguez House, where the local militia met, are evidence that the attack involved not only soldiers but Columbus residents. The depot has been used as a library, a newspaper office, and a meeting place for local Boy Scouts; it is now a historical museum. The nearby customs house is now Pancho Villa State Park's museum and visitor center.

A sign on the railroad station door often says "closed/cerrado," a reminder that Columbus is rooted in its border-town history. With ten thousand residents, Palomas, its sister city across the border, overshadows the sleepy community, which has fewer than two thousand residents.

CHAPTER SEVENTEEN

Texas–New Mexico Railway

Toot and Never Move

Southeastern New Mexico was primarily dedicated to stock raising until oil was discovered in 1927. The Texas–New Mexico Railway, or TNM, a subsidiary of the Texas & Pacific, was incorporated that year to build a line to serve both the cattle and oil industries in Lea County. Construction began in 1928 from Monahans, Texas, on the Texas & Pacific Railway, and tracks reached Lovington, 112 miles north, on July 20, 1930. In 1933, the TNM leased one locomotive, one freight car, and one passenger car. Even at its inception, the railroad was primarily for freight; in 1952, passenger revenues totaled only $56, while freight revenues were more than $1.2 million.

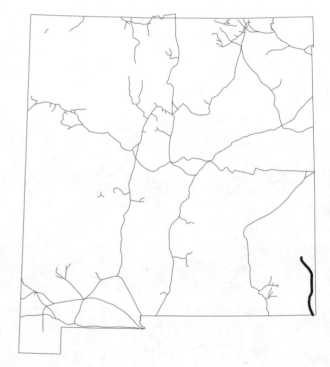

The only depot in New Mexico remaining from the line, once affectionately known as the Toot and Never Move, is the Hobbs depot. The area was settled by a Texas family named Hobbs, and though they applied for a post office requesting that the town be called Taft or Prairieview, the postal officials accidentally substituted the family name. The large depot, similar to Texan stations on the line, was built in 1928. Though it had minimal ornamentation, it featured a semioctagonal recessed porch that allowed for all exterior doors to be concentrated in one location. The depot was retired in 1978, purchased in 1982, moved to Lovington, and converted to a residence.

PART FIVE

APPENDICES

Remaining Railroad Structures in New Mexico

The process of identifying and cataloging historic railroad buildings is ongoing. Therefore, this list of remaining railroad structures in New Mexico is not comprehensive. Railroad depots and section houses that were constructed of wood frame were intentionally easy to relocate; when railroads abandoned lines and sold structures, the structures were hauled away and converted to new uses. The result is that the structures that were previously thought to be lost are sometimes found in private hands.

There are rumors of railroad depots in several locations. The Dexter depot may be in Roswell; it was once an adult bookstore. There is a rumor that the El Monero depot is a restaurant in Dulce. The Taylor Springs depot is on the Sauble Ranch in Abbott. It is unclear if Magdalena's first depot, constructed in 1885, still exists as a private residence on Chestnut Street. Other depots are said to be private homes, including the Farley depot (which may now be in Sofia), the French depot (which may be in Springer), the Springer depot (in Edgewood), the Fierro depot, and the Texico depot. The Yeso depot is said to be in Vaughn. Section houses dot the landscape of New Mexico and many are not included in this book. There is a section house in Stanley, and there may be others in Rincon. In addition,

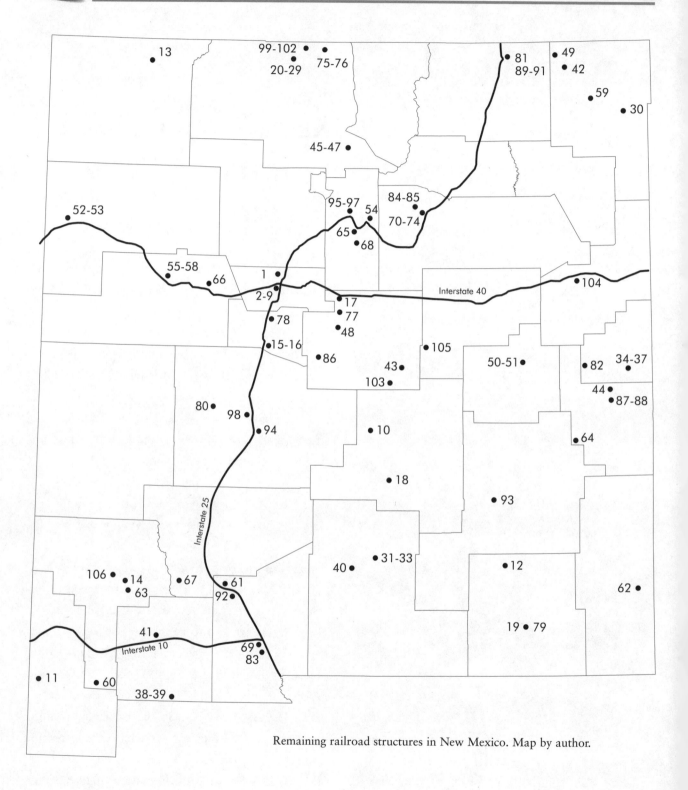

Remaining railroad structures in New Mexico. Map by author.

there are other structures such as water tanks and bridges that are not listed here.

Furthermore, some structures in this book may no longer exist; railroad buildings often succumb to neglect or are demolished.

The following table is numbered to correspond to map 16, locating remaining railroad buildings and other structures in New Mexico. They are listed by

historic location. In some cases, a building was relocated and served more than one location; in this case, the historic location is the place most associated with that building. Other historic locations are listed. It is also identified whether or not the structure was relocated after retirement. Although current uses are listed, these tend to change often.

Map No.	Historic Location	Other Location	Relocated	Type	Constructed by	Year Constructed	Current use
1	Abajo	—	Yes	Depot	ATSF	1886	Office
2	Albuquerque	—	No	Curio Storage Bldg.	ATSF	1912	Depot
3	Albuquerque	—	No	Telegraph bldg.	ATSF	1914	Railroad (vacant)
4	Albuquerque	—	No	Freight depot	ATSF	1946	Railroad
5	Albuquerque	—	No	Fire station	ATSF	1920	Railroad (vacant)
6	Albuquerque	—	No	Machine shop	ATSF	1921	Railroad (vacant)
7	Albuquerque	—	No	Boiler shop	ATSF	1922	Railroad (vacant)
8	Albuquerque	—	No	Various shops	ATSF	ca. 1917	Railroad (vacant)
9	Albuquerque	—	No	Railroad hospital	ATSF	1926	Hospital
10	Ancho	—	Yes	Depot	EPNE	1902	Museum
11	Animas	—	Yes	Depot	EPSW	1902	Residence
12	Artesia	—	No	Depot	ATSF	ca. 1912	Chamber of commerce / Visitor center
13	Aztec	—	Yes	Depot	DRG	1915	Residence
14	Bayard	—	No	Depot	ATSF	1915	Storage
15	Belen	—	No	Depot	ATSF	1909	Railroad
16	Belen	—	No	Harvey House	ATSF	ca. 1909	Museum
17	Calvert/Moriarty	—	No	Depot	SFC	1903	Church
18	Capitan (1906)	Coalora (1900)	No	Depot	EPNE	1900	Vacant
19	Carlsbad	—	No	Depot	ATSF	1904	Railroad
20	Chama	—	No	Depot	DRG	1899	Depot
21	Chama	—	No	Water tower	DRG	1897	Water tower
22	Chama	—	No	Roundhouse	DRG	1899	Repair shop
23	Chama	—	No	Coal tipple	DRG	1924	Coal tipple
24	Chama	—	No	Stock pens	DRG	1880s	Railroad (vacant)
25	Chama	—	No	Bunkhouse	DRG	1880s	Railroad (vacant)
26	Chama	—	No	Sand house	DRG	Unknown	Sand house
27	Chama	—	No	Ash pit	DRG	Unknown	Ash pit
28	Chama	—	No	Oil house	DRG	1903	Oil house
29	Chama	—	No	Track scale	DRG	1929	Railroad (vacant)
30	Clayton	—	No	Depot	ATSF	1931	Residence
31	Cloudcroft	—	No	Lodge	EPNE	1911	Hotel
32	Cloudcroft	—	No	Pavilion	EPNE	1923	Hotel
33	Cloudcroft	—	No	Trestle	EPNE	1899	End of Trail

Coalora (see Capitan no. 18)

Map No.	Historic Location	Other Location	Moved?	Type	Constructed by	Year Constructed	Current use
34	Clovis	—	No	Depot	ATSF	1907	Museum
35	Clovis	—	No	Harvey House	ATSF	ca. 1909	Railroad (vacant)
36	Clovis	—	No	Office bldg.	ATSF	1920	Railroad (vacant)
37	Clovis	—	No	Turntable	ATSF	ca. 1907	Railroad (vacant)
38	Columbus	—	No	Depot	EPSW	1902	Museum
39	Columbus	—	No	Customs house	—	1902	Museum
40	Corona	Torrance (1899)	Yes	Depot	EPNE	1899	Museum
41	Deming	—	No	Depot/Hotel	SP	1881	Railroad
42	Des Moines	—	Maybe	Depot	ATSF	1880s	Residence
43	Duran	—	Yes	Depot	EPNE	ca. 1902	Residence
44	Elida	—	Yes	Depot	ATSF	1910	Residence
45	Embudo	—	No	Depot	DRG	1880	Residence
46	Embudo	—	No	Freight house	DRG	ca. 1880	Residence
47	Embudo	—	No	Water tank	DRG	Unknown	Vacant
48	Estancia (1951)	Lucy (1908)	Yes	Depot	ATSF	1908	Residence (vacant)
49	Folsom	—	Yes	Depot	DTFW	1888	Residence
50	Fort Sumner	—	No	Depot	ATSF	1908	Railroad
51	Fort Sumner	—	No	Bridge	ATSF	1905–1908	Railroad
52	Gallup	—	No	Depot	ATSF	1923	Depot/Cultural center
53	Gallup	—	No	Maintenance bldg.	ATSF	Unknown	Railroad (vacant)
54	Glorieta	—	No	Depot	ATSF	1927	Post office
55	Grants	—	No	Depot	ATSF	Unknown	Railroad
56	Grants	—	No	Toolhouse	ATSF	Unknown	Railroad
57	Grants (Breece)	—	No	Engine house	B	1920s	Lumberyard
58	Grants (Breece)	—	No	Company housing	B	1920s	Vacant
59	Grenville	—	Maybe	Depot	FWDC	1880s	Residence
60	Hachita	—	Yes	Depot	EPSW	1902	Vacant
61	Hatch (1936)	San Marcial (1930) new site	Depot	ATSF	1930	Library/Museum
62	Hobbs	—	Yes	Depot	TNM	1928	Residence
63	Hurley	—	No	Depot	ATSF	1911	Railroad
64	Kenna	—	Yes	Depot	ATSF	1911	Residence
65	Kennedy	—	Yes	Depot	ATSF	1907	Clubhouse
66	Laguna	—	No	Depot	ATSF	ca. 1880	Residence
67	Lake Valley	—	No	Depot	ATSF	1885	Vacant
68	Lamy	—	No	Depot	ATSF	1909	Depot
69	Las Cruces	—	No	Depot	ATSF	1910	City of Las Cruces
70	Las Vegas	—	No	Depot	ATSF	1898	Depot/Intermodal
71	Las Vegas	—	No	Harvey House	ATSF	1899	Vacant
72	Las Vegas	—	No	Harvey House dormitory	—	1899	Vacant
73	Las Vegas	—	No	Freight depot	ATSF	1926	Railroad (vacant)
74	Las Vegas	—	No	Roundhouse	ATSF	1917	Vacant
75	Lava	—	No	Pump house	DRG	1890s	Railroad (vacant)
76	Lava	—	No	Water tower	DRG	1918	Water tower
77	Los Cerrillos	—	Yes	Depot	ATSF	1882	Residence
78	Los Lunas	—	Yes	Depot	ATSF	1879	City storage
79	Loving (1946)	Orla, Tex. (1910), Angeles, Tex. (1935)	Yes	Depot	ATSF	1910	Vacant

Lucy (see Estancia, no. 48)

No.	Map Location	Historic Location	Other	Moved?	Type Constructed by	Year Constructed	Current use
80	Magdalena	—	No	Depot	ATSF	1915	Library/City office
81	Maxwell	—	Yes	Depot	ATSF	1909	Residence
82	Melrose	—	No	Depot	ATSF	1907	Railroad
83	Mesilla Park	—	No	Depot	ATSF	1925	Railroad
84	Montezuma	—	No	Hotel	ATSF	ca. 1886	Conference center
85	Montezuma	—	No	Powerhouse	ATSF	Unknown	Vacant
86	Mountainair	—	No	Depot	ATSF	1908	Railroad
87	Portales	—	No	Depot	ATSF	1913	Storage
88	Portales	—	No	Icehouse	ATSF	ca. 1928	Retail
89	Raton	—	No	Depot	ATSF	1904	Depot
90	Raton	—	No	Railroad Express	ATSF	ca. 1912	Gallery
91	Raton	—	No	Freight depot	ATSF	1903	Railroad
92	Rincon	—	No	Depot	ATSF	1884	Railroad
93	Roswell	—	No	Depot (freight port)	ATSF	1905	Railroad (vacant)
94	San Antonio	—	Yes	Depot (freight port)	ATSF	1882	Vacant
San Marcial (see Hatch, no. 61)							
95	Santa Fe	—	No	Depot	ATSF	1909	Depot
96	Santa Fe	—	No	Hotel	ATSF	1920	Hotel
97	Santa Fe	—	No	Depot	SFC	ca. 1903	Restaurant
98	Socorro	—	No	Depot	ATSF	1888	Railroad
99	Sublette	—	No	Standpipe/Concrete reservoir	DRG	1939	Water provision
100	Sublette	—	No	Bunkhouse	DRG	1880s	Railroad (vacant)
101	Sublette	—	No	Bunkhouse	DRG	Unknown	Railroad (vacant)
102	Sublette	—	No	Section house	DRG	Unknown	Railroad (vacant)
103	Torrance	—	Yes	Depot (freight port)	SFC	1903	Storage
104	Tucumcari	—	No	Depot	CRIP	1926	Railroad
105	Vaughn	—	No	Depot	ATSF	1908	Railroad
106	Whitewater	—	No	Depot	ATSF	1884	Residence

Abbreviations for Railroads:

ATSF	Atchison, Topeka & Santa Fe (Santa Fe Railway)
B	Breece Company
CRIP	Chicago, Rock Island & Pacific (El Paso)
DRG	Denver & Rio Grande
DTFW	Dallas, Texas & Fort Worth
EPNE	El Paso & Northeastern
EPSW	El Paso & Southwestern
FWDC	Fort Worth & Denver City
SFC	Santa Fe Central
SP	Southern Pacific
TNM	Texas–New Mexico

APPENDIX TWO

Heritage Tourism

The following table, corresponding by number to map 16, indicates current location as well as ownership and access considerations. Visiting historic structures is informative and interesting, but please use caution, good judgment, and common sense on your visits.

1. Ownership of railroad-related properties varies greatly. Though some properties are open to the public, it is advisable to call ahead for hours of operation. Many properties are privately owned; though some can be viewed from public property or rights-of-way, please respect the privacy of private home and business owners. Do not trespass.

2. Railroad tracks are private railroad property; in addition, they can be very dangerous. Many depots are adjacent to main lines and active sidings.

3. Ownership inevitably changes over time. What was once an accessible, public building may now be private property.

4. Do not remove any property or features. Even if a building is currently derelict, these features could be important to a later preservation effort.

No.	Current name	Access	Address
1	Plaza San Ysidro	P, E	4767 Corrales Rd., Corrales
2	Albuquerque Amtrak station	O	214 First St. SW, Albuquerque
3	Former telegraph bldg.	R, E	First St. SW, Albuquerque
4	Albuquerque freight house	R, E	First St. SW, Albuquerque
5	Former fire station	R, V	Second St. SW, Albuquerque
6	Former machine shop	R, V	Second St. SW (north of Pacific), Albuquerque
7	Former boiler shop	R, V	Second St. SW (north of Pacific), Albuquerque
8	Former railroad shops	R, V	Second St. SW (north of Pacific), Albuquerque
9	Memorial Hospital	P, E	806 Central Ave., Albuquerque
10	My House of Old Things	O	2 miles off U.S. Highway 54, Ancho
11	Former Animas depot	P	Private residence
12	Artesia Chamber of Commerce	O	107 N. First St., Artesia
13	Former Aztec depot	P	Private residence
14	Former Bayard depot	P, V	Central Ave. and Coffey St., Bayard
15	Belen depot	R, V	106 N. First St., Belen
16	Belen Harvey House	O	104 N. First St., Belen
17	Our Lady of Mt. Carmel Church	P, V	Highway 41, Moriarty
18	Former Capitan depot	P, E	Corner State Road 246/48 and U.S. Highway 380, Capitan
19	Former Carlsbad depot	R, V	End of E. Fox St., Carlsbad
20	Cumbres & Toltec depot	O	500 Terrace Ave., Chama
21	Cumbres & Toltec water tower	R, E	500 Terrace Ave., Chama

22	Cumbres & Toltec roundhouse	R, E	500 Terrace Ave., Chama
23	Cumbres & Toltec coal tipple	R, E	500 Terrace Ave., Chama
24	Former Chama stock pens	R, V	500 Terrace Ave., Chama
25	Former Chama bunkhouse	R, E	500 Terrace Ave., Chama
26	Cumbres & Toltec sand house	R, E	500 Terrace Ave., Chama
27	Cumbres & Toltec ash pit	R, E	500 Terrace Ave., Chama
28	Cumbres & Toltec oil house	R, E	500 Terrace Ave., Chama
29	Former Chama track scale	R, E	500 Terrace Ave., Chama
30	Former Clayton depot	P	Private residence
31	The Lodge at Cloudcroft	O	1 Corona Pl., Cloudcroft
32	The Pavilion	P, E	Corner of Chipmunk Ave. and Curlew Pl., Cloudcroft
33	Mexican Trestle	O	U.S. Highway 82, Cloudcroft
34	Clovis Depot Model Train Museum	O	221 W. First St., Clovis
35	Former Gran Quivira	R, V	W. First St., Clovis
36	Former Clovis Office Bldg.	R, V	W. First St., Clovis
37	Former Clovis turntable	R, V	Railyard, Clovis
38	Columbus Historical Society Museum	O	Intersection of State Roads 9 and 11, Columbus
39	Pancho Villa State Park	O	Intersection of State Roads 9 and 11, Columbus
40	The Toy Train Depot	O	1991 N. White Sands Blvd., Alamogordo
41	Former Deming depot/hotel	R, V	301 E. Railroad Ave., Deming
42	Former Des Moines depot	P	Private residence
43	Former Duran depot	P	Private residence
44	Former Elida depot	P	Private residence
45	Embudo Station	P, E	State Road 68, Embudo
46	Embudo freight house	P, E	State Road 68, Embudo
47	Embudo water tank	P, E	State Road 68, Embudo
48	Former Estancia depot	P	Private residence
49	Former Folsom depot	P	Private residence
50	Former Fort Sumner depot	R, V	Santa Fe Ave., Fort Sumner
51	Fort Sumner bridge	R, V	Highway 60 west
52	Gallup depot	O	201 E. Highway 66, Gallup
53	Gallup maintenance bldg.	R, V	Railyard, Gallup
54	Glorieta Post Office	O	Off Firestation Rd., over tracks, rt. Calle Lonia
55	Former Grants depot	R, V	State Road 122, Grants
56	Former Grants toolhouse	R, V	State Road 122, Grants
57	Diamond G Lumber	P, V	225 El Morro Rd., Grants
58	Former Breece Co. housing	P, V	Adjacent to 225 El Morro Rd, Grants
59	Former Grenville depot	P	Private residence
60	Former Hachita depot	P	Private residence
61	Hatch Public Library	O	503 E. Hall, Hatch
62	Former Hobbs depot	P	Private residence
63	Hurley depot	R, V	End of Cortez St., Hurley
64	Former Kenna depot	P	Private residence
65	Eldorado Clubhouse	P, E	1 Hacienda Loop, Eldorado
66	Former Laguna depot	P	Private residence
67	Former Lake Valley depot	P	Railroad St./Ave., Lake Valley
68	Lamy depot	O	County Road 33 (center of town), Lamy
69	Las Cruces depot	P, E	800 W. Las Cruces Ave. (end of Mesilla St.), Las Cruces

70	Las Vegas depot	O	Railroad Ave. (end of E. Lincoln St.), Las Vegas
71	Former La Castañeda	P, V	524 Railroad Ave., Las Vegas
72	Rawlins bldg.	P, V	515 Railroad Ave., Las Vegas
73	Former Las Vegas freight depot	P, V	Railroad Ave., Las Vegas
74	Former Las Vegas roundhouse	P, V	End of Railroad Ave., Las Vegas
75	Former Lava pump house	P, V	Adjacent to Los Pinos Creek, Lava
76	Lava water tower	R, V	Adjacent to railroad, Lava
77	Former Los Cerrillos depot	P	Private residence
78	Former Los Lunas depot	P, V	State Road 314, Los Lunas
79	Former Loving depot	P, V	2820 Standpipe Rd., Carlsbad
80	Magdalena Village Hall	O	108 N. Main St.
81	Former Maxwell depot	P	Private residence
82	Former Melrose depot	R, V	U.S. Highway 60, Melrose
83	Former Mesilla Park depot	R, V	Highway 478 (E. Main St. and Conway Ave.), Las Cruces
84	Former Montezuma Hotel	Og	State Road 65, Montezuma
85	Former Montezuma powerhouse	P, V	State Road 65, Montezuma
86	Former Mountainair depot	R, V	End of Main St., Mountainair
87	Former Portales depot	R, V	End of Avenue A at railroad tracks, Portales
88	Portales icehouse	P, V	Avenue A, Portales
89	Raton depot	O	201 S. First St. (at intersection of Cook St.), Raton
90	Old Pass Gallery	O	145 S. First St., Raton
91	Former Raton freight depot	R, V	First St., Raton
92	Former Rincon depot	R, V	Rincon Rd., Rincon
93	Former Roswell depot	R, V	Railroad Ave. and E. Fifth St., Roswell
94	Former San Antonio depot	P, V	Main St., south of U.S. Highway 380, San Antonio
95	Santa Fe Southern depot	O	410 S. Guadalupe St., Santa Fe
96	La Fonda Hotel	O	100 E. San Francisco St., Santa Fe
97	Tomasita's Restaurant	O	500 S. Guadalupe St., Santa Fe
98	Former Socorro depot	R, V	End of Manzanares Ave. E., Socorro
99	Sublette Standpipe/Concrete reservoir	R, V	Sublette
100	Former Sublette bunkhouse	R, V	Sublette
101	Former Sublette bunkhouse	R, V	Sublette
102	Former Sublette section house	R, V	Sublette
103	Former Torrance depot	P	Private residence
104	Former Tucumcari depot	R, V	Main St., Tucumcari
105	Former Vaughn depot	R, V	U.S. Highway 54, Vaughn
106	Former Whitewater depot	P	Private residence

Abbreviations for Ownership/Access:

O—Open to public; interior and exterior access; check hours of operation
Og—Open to public; interior and exterior access; guided tours only, call ahead
P—Private residence; no access
P, E—Privately owned; exterior access only
P, V—Privately owned; exterior viewed from public property/right of way only
R, E—Railroad owned; exterior access only
R, V—Railroad owned private property; exterior viewed from public property/right of way only

APPENDIX THREE

Useful Contacts

Planning Assistance

National Trust for Historic Preservation
Southwest Regional Office
500 Main Street, Suite 1030
Fort Worth, TX 76102
(817) 332–4398
http://www.nationaltrust.org/

New Mexico Office of Cultural Affairs—
        Historic Preservation Division
Room 320, La Villa Rivera
228 East Palace Avenue
Santa Fe, NM 87501
(505) 827–6320
http://www.museums.state.nm.us/hpd/

New Mexico State Highway and Transportation
Department—Intermodal Division
1120 Cerrillos Road, P.O. Box 1149
Santa Fe, NM 87504–1149
(505) 827–5100
http://nmshtd.state.nm.us/general/depts/tpd/rr/default.asp

Reconnecting America (formerly Great American
        Station Foundation)
615 East Lincoln Avenue
Las Vegas, NM 87701
(505) 426–8055
http://www.reconnectingamerica.org/

Associations (Railroads and Historical)

National Association of Railroad Passengers (NARP)
900 Second Street NE, Suite 308
Washington, DC 20002–3557
(202) 408–8362
http://www.narprail.org/

National Railway Historical Society
100 North 17th Street
Philadelphia, PA 19103
(215) 557–6606
http://www.nrhs.com

Railroad Station Historical Society
http://www.rrshs.org/

Railway and Locomotive Historical Society
http://www.rrhistorical-2.com/rlhs/
Southwest chapter
http://trainweb.org/ep-sw/index1.htm

APPENDIX FOUR

Railroad-Related Museums in New Mexico

Clovis Depot Model Train Museum
(in the Clovis depot)
221 West First Street
Clovis, NM 88101
(505) 762–0066 or (888) 762–0064
http://www.clovisdepot.com/

Columbus Historical Society Museum
(in the Columbus depot)
Intersection of State Roads 9 and 11
Columbus, NM 88029
(505) 531–2620
http://www.nmculture.org/cgi-
bin/instview.cgi?_recordnum=COLU

Cumbres & Toltec Scenic Railroad
(in the Chama depot and railyard)
500 Terrace Avenue
Chama, NM 87520
(505) 756–2151
http://www.cumbrestoltec.com

Montezuma Hotel
Armand Hammer United World College
Montezuma, NM 87731
(505) 454–4221
http://www.uwc-usa.org/reopening.htm
(Guided tours only—see Web site and call for times)

My House of Old Things
two miles off U.S. Highway 54
Ancho, NM 88301
(505) 648–2546
(Open May to October)

Pancho Villa State Park
(in the Columbus custom's house)
Intersection of State Roads 9 and 11
Columbus, NM 88029
(505) 531–2711

Santa Fe Southern Railway
(in the Santa Fe depot)
410 South Guadalupe Street
Santa Fe, NM 87501
(888) 989–8600
http://www.sfsr.com

The Toy Train Depot
(in the Corona depot)
1991 North White Sands Blvd.
Alamogordo, NM 88310
(505) 437–2855 or (888) 207–3564
http://www.toytraindepot.homestead.com/

Valencia County Historical Society's Harvey House
Museum
(in the Belen Harvey House)
104 North First Street
Belen, NM 87002
(505) 861–0581
http://www.nmculture.org/cgi-
bin/instview.cgi?_recordnum=HARV

Wheels
700 Silver SW
Albuquerque, NM 87103
(505) 243–6269
http://www.wheelsmuseum.org/

Notes

Chapter 1

1. Bob Parsons, telephone conversation with author, August 7, 2003.

Chapter 2

1. *Quarterly Review* (March 1825): 361–62.

2. Henry Booth, *Account of the Liverpool and Manchester Railway* (Liverpool: Wales and Barnes, 1830).

3. William R. King, "The Congressional Globe," 31st. Cong., 1st sess., April 29, 1850, 845–46.

4. Quoted in Rowan House, "It's About Time," *L & N Magazine* (February 1963):12.

5. Frank Norris, *The Octopus: A Story of California* (Doubleday, Page, 1901).

Chapter 3

1. Quoted in Thomas Christensen et al., *The U.S.–Mexican War* (Dallas: KERA-TV, 1998).

Chapter 8

1. *Chief Way Reference Standards, Santa Fe System Standards*, vol. 2 (Dallas: Kachina Press, 1978).

2. Charles Fletcher Lummis, "In the Lion's Den," *Land of Sunshine* (December 1895): 43.

3. Charles Fletcher Lummis, "In the Lion's Den," *Land of Sunshine* (January 1896): 89.

Chapter 9

1. Quoted in Diane H. Thomas, *The Southwestern Indian Detours: The Story of the Fred Harvey/Santa Fe Railway Experiment in "Detourism"* (Phoenix: Hunter, 1978).

2. "Social Centers for Railroad Men," *Chautauquan Magazine* (June 1904).

Chapter 12

1. National Park Service, "National Register Bulletin 16A: How to Complete the National Register Registration Form, Part II: Getting Started," Washington, D.C.: U.S. Department of the Interior, 1997.

Chapter 13

1. C. M. Chase, *The Editor's Run in New Mexico and Colorado* (1882; Ft. Davis, Tex.: Frontier, 1968), 138–39.

2. Quoted in F. Stanley, *The Magdalena, New Mexico Story* (Nazareth, Tex.: privately printed, 1973), 8.

3. Don McAlovy, telephone conversation with author, August 1, 2003.

4. Quoted in F. Stanley, *The Clovis, New Mexico Story* (Pampa, Tex.: privately printed, 1966), 14.

5. J. M. Meade (chief engineer of the Atchison, Topeka & Santa Fe), ed., "Meade's Manual," Russell L. Crump, ca. 1920.

6. Quoted in F. Stanley, *The Carlsbad, New Mexico Story* (Pep, Tex.: privately printed, 1963).

7. Quoted in Stanley, *Carlsbad, New Mexico*, 17.

8. John S. Phelps, Speech welcoming the President and directors of the Atlantic & Pacific Railroad to Springfield, May 3, 1870.

9. Quoted in Christopher Huggard, "Mining and the Environment: The Clean Air Issue in New Mexico, 1960–1980," *New Mexico Historical Review* 69 (October 1994): 369–88.

Chapter 14

1. "Farewell to 'Chile Line': Denver and Rio Grande's Last Passenger Train Runs Today," *Albuquerque Tribune*, September 1, 1941.

2. "Embudo Depot: A Picture Done in Rocks," *Denver & Rio Grande Magazine* (July 1926).

Chapter 16

1. Quoted in F. Stanley, *The Deming, New Mexico Story* (Pantex, Tex.: privately printed, 1966), 6.

2. *Santa Fe New Mexican*, October 21, 1897.

3. G. Anderson, *History of New Mexico* (Los Angeles: Pacific, 1907) and 1901.

Glossary

Adobe—Traditional southwestern building material consisting of clay mixed with water and straw and formed into blocks.

Arcade—A roofed walkway with a series of arched openings on one side.

Base—The lower portion of an exterior wall, which often projects from the facade.

Battered walls—Walls with inclined faces where the bottom of the wall is thicker than the top.

Board and batten—Exterior siding in which the seams between vertical wood boards are covered with vertical battens, narrower wood strips.

Bracketed cornice—A cornice incorporating small brackets that appear to support roof eaves.

Brackets—Structural members extending from walls to support overhanging roof eaves.

Buttress—A thickened portion of a wall used to brace its lateral movement.

Canal—Overflow scupper projecting from the facade of Spanish and Mexican buildings that drains excess rainwater from the roof while preventing water from damaging exterior walls.

Clapboard—Exterior siding in which tapered horizontal boards (thicker on their bottom edges) are lapped to shed rain and snow.

Coping—The top course of a wall or parapet (usually masonry).

Cornice—Projected molding at the top of a wall or facade.

Crenelated—Having a series of square indentations.

Cross-gable—A gabled roof intersecting another gabled roof. The ridges are perpendicular to each other.

Doric column—Simplest of the ancient Greek column types, Doric columns have a simple capital, the top of the column.

Dormer—A window projecting from a sloping roof with its own roof, often a cross-gable.

Double-hung window—A window with two sashes that slide vertically past each other to provide an opening at either the top or bottom.

Eaves—The portion of a roof that projects beyond the exterior wall of a building.

Facade—An exterior wall of a building.

Fish scale shingles—Shingles with decorative rounded bottoms.

Frame construction—A construction system in which structural supports are made of wood framing.

Frieze—A decorative band near the top of a wall or above an opening.

Gable—A triangular area on each end of a building formed by two sloping roofs.

Gabled roof—A double sloping roof forming a gable on each end.

Hipped roof—A roof that slopes on all four sides.

Lintel—A horizontal support spanning a door or window opening to transfer the load to walls or columns on either side.

Masonry construction—A construction system using cementitious materials such as stone, brick, concrete, concrete blocks, or a combination of these.

Mull—To join windows together at the jamb, head, or sill, or to join door-side lights to the door jambs.

Mullion—The members joining panes of glass in divided windows.

Parapet—A vertical extension of a wall above the roofline.

Pediment—A triangular gable above a cornice.

Pilaster—A rectangular column projecting from a wall.

Plat—To map a town or subdivision with boundaries of individual properties identified.

Plaza—Spanish or Spanish Colonial town square.

Portal—A porch supported by columns across the facade of a building.

Quatrefoil—An ornamental shape with four lobes (called foils).

Quoins—A series of alternating large and small masonry units—stones or blocks—along the full height of the outside corners of a building, used for reinforcement and/or accenting the building corners.

Remate—A wall that projects above the roof to make a building appear taller or more substantial. The parapet of a remate is often curved.

Sash—A window unit, often operable, inside a window frame.

Scissor brackets—Brackets in which the central members cross each other at an angle similar to a pair of scissors.

String course—A thin horizontal molding in a continuous row on the facade of a building.

Veneer—A nonstructural material applied to the exterior of a building.

Bibliography

A & K Railroad Materials, Inc. Available at www.akrail-road.com/track_asssemble.html.

Anderson, G. *History of New Mexico*. Los Angeles: Pacific States Publishing Company, 1907.

Armstrong, John H. *The Railroad, What It Is, What It Does*. Omaha: Simmons-Boardman Books, Inc., 1977.

Armstrong, Ruth. "One Hundred Years of Railroad Towns." *New Mexico Magazine* (April 1980): 4.

———. "Riley's Switch." *New Mexico Magazine* (April 1980): 44–46.

———. "Six Shooter Siding." *New Mexico Magazine* (April 1980): 8–10.

Beck, Warren A. and Ynez D. Aase. *Historical Atlas of New Mexico*. Norman and London: University of Oklahoma Press, 1969.

Berke, Arnold. "Drawing from the Desert." *Preservation Magazine*. July/August 1977, p. 34–43.

Brooker, Kathleen. "Railroad Depots in New Mexico: Southwestern Styles and the Masonry Tradition." Thesis, Master of Architecture. Albuquerque: University of New Mexico, May 1981.

Bryant, Keith L., Jr. *History of the Atchison, Topeka and Santa Fe Railway*. Lincoln and London: University of Nebraska Press, 1974.

Burlington Northern Santa Fe. "BNSF History." Available at www.bnsf.com/about_bnsf/html/history.html.

Burroughs, Jean M. "'Pea Vine' Railroad: Lifeline of the Prairie." *Greater Llano Estacado Southwest Heritage* 5, no. 2 (summer 1975): 14–17.

Burton, Bob. "A Branch Line comes of Age." Originally appeared in *Santa Fe Modeler* 12, no. 1 (1989). Available at www.atsfrr.com/resources/burton/branch-2.htm.

Chan, I. Meg, ed. *Building on the Past, Traveling to the Future: A Preservationist's Guide to the ITEA Transportation Enhancement Provision*. Federal Highway Administration and National Trust for Historic Preservation, 1994.

The Chief Way Reference Series System Standards: Volume Two. Pamphlet. Dallas: Kachina Press, 1978.

Citizens Guide to ISTEA. Washington, D.C.: Transit and Rail Funding and Public Participation Requirements Campaign for New Transportation Priorities, National Association of Railroad Passengers, May 1993.

"Coffeyville Bricks." City of Coffeyville, Kansas. Available at www.coffeyville.com/History.htm.

Combs, John. "Mechanical Reefer." Available at www.alaskarails.org/fp/mech-reefers.html. 2000.

Coop's Road Map Guide to Western Railroads and Railroad Museums. Menlo Park, Calif.: Lone Mountain Designs, 1996.

Crump, Russell. *Selections from Meade's Manual*. Available at http://www.atsfry.com/EasternArchive/Meades/.

"Deming Had Role in Railroad Mail." *Albuquerque Journal*, November 27, 1969.

Dorman, Richard L. *The Chili Line and Santa Fe, the City Different*. Santa Fe: RD Publications, 2000.

Eddy, John A. and Charles B. Eddy. *John A. and Charles B. Eddy Collection 1897–1990*. Fray Angelico Chavez History Library, Santa Fe.

"Embudo Depot: A Picture Done in Rocks." *Denver & Rio Grande Western Magazine* 2, no. 9 (July 1926).

Engineering and Technology Department. Route Familiarization Chart: Central Region, Gallup and Glorieta Subdivisions. Pamphlet. February 1992.

Escott, George S. *History and Directory of Springfield and North Springfield*. Springfield, Mo.: Office of the Patriot-Advertiser, 1878.

"Farewell to 'Chili Line': Denver and Rio Grande's Last Passenger Train Runs Today." *Albuquerque Tribune*, September 1, 1941.

Fleming, Elvis. "James John Hagerman: Building the Pecos Valley Railroad." *Greater Llano Estacado Southwest Heritage* 7, no. 1 (spring 1977): 6–12.

Fleming, R. "Chili Line." *New Mexico Magazine* (November 1941): 24, 40.

Fugate, Francis L. and Roberta B. Fugate. *Roadside History of New Mexico*. Missoula, Mont.: Mountain Press Publishing Company, 1989.

Glover, V. "New Mexico Central." *New Mexico Magazine* (June 1975): 22–23.

Glover, Vernon. *Logging Railroads of the Lincoln National Forest, New Mexico*. U.S. Department of Agriculture, Forest Service, Southwest Region Report #4, September 1984.

Glover, Vernon and Joseph P. Hereford, Jr. *Zuni Mountain Railroads, Cibola National Forest, New Mexico*. Historical Society of New Mexico, 1986.

Glover, Vernon and Wilson & Company. *Inventory of Branch Line Railroads in New Mexico*. Report. Santa Fe: New Mexico State Highway and Transportation Department, May 1993.

Grant, H. Roger. *Living in the Depot: The Two-Story Railroad Station*. Iowa City: University of Iowa Press, 1993.

Halberstadt, Hans and April Halberstadt. *Great American Train Stations*. New York: Barnes and Noble Books, 1997.

Hankey, John P. "America's Oldest Depot." *Locomotive and Railway Preservation* (May–June 1996): n.p.

Henry, R. S. "The Railroad Land Grant Legend in American History Texts." *Mississipi Valley Historical Review* 32, no. 2 (September 1945): 171–94.

Herron, G. "Saving the Belen Harvey House." *New Mexico Magazine* (June 1986): 24–27.

How to Apply the National Register Criteria for Evaluation. Washington, D.C.: U.S. Department of the Interior, National Park Service, Interagency Resources Division, 1991.

Howard, Kathleen L. and Diana F. Pardue. *Inventing the Southwest: The Fred Harvey Company and Native American Art*. Flagstaff: Northland Publishing, 1996.

Howse, Rowan. "It's About Time!" *L. & N. Magazine* 39, no. 2 (February 1963): 12.

Huggard, Christopher. "Mining and the Environment: The Clean Air Issue in New Mexico 1960–1980." *New Mexico Historical Review* 69 (October 1994): 369–88.

"Interstate Commerce Commission." *The Columbia Encyclopedia*, sixth ed. New York: Columbia University Press, 2003. Available at www.bartleby.com/65/.

Julyan, Robert. *The Place Names of New Mexico*. Albuquerque: University of New Mexico Press, 1996.

Lee, Sally J., Tina L. Powell, Todd Agthe, and Neal W. Ackerly (Center for Anthropological Research, New Mexico State University). *Historic Buildings in the Alameda Depot Historic Area*. Report. Barton-Aschman Associates, Inc., n.d.

Lippmann, Lionel and Virginia Watson-Jones. *Capitan, New Mexico: 1900–2000*. Capitan: Friends of Smokey–Capitan, Inc., 2000.

Looney, Ralph. *Haunted Highways: The Ghost Towns of New Mexico*. Albuquerque: University of New Mexico Press, 1968.

Mazria Associates, Inc. *Railroad Depots of New Mexico*. Report. Santa Fe: New Mexico State Highway and Transportation Division, Intermodal Management Bureau, 1996.

Mazria Associates, Inc. and Avraham Shama and Associates. *Market Analysis and Architectural Design for the Conversion of Santa Fe Railway Depots at Gallup, Raton and Las Vegas to Intermodal Transportation Facilities*. Report. Santa Fe: New Mexico State Highway and Transportation Department, 1987.

Meeks, Carroll L. V. *The Railroad Station: An Architectural History*. 1956. Reprint, New York: Dover Publications, Inc., 1995.

Montoya, Margaret. "They Remember the Chili Line." *The Taos News*. June 9, 1966: 5.

Myrick, David E. *New Mexico's Railroads: A Historical Survey*. Albuquerque: University of New Mexico Press, 1970 (revised 1990).

National Park Service. *National Register Bulletin—How to Complete the National Register Registration Form*. Available at http://www.cr.nps.gov/nr/publications/bulletins/nrb16a/nrb16a_II.htm.

"New Mexico and its Railroads." *New Mexico Railroader* no. 178 (August 1989): 1–4.

Noble, David Grant. *Pueblos, Villages, Forts and Trails: A Guide to New Mexico's Past*. Albuquerque: University of New Mexico Press, 1994.

Norris, Frank. *The Octopus: A Story of California*. 1901. Reprint, New York: Penguin Books, 1986.

Oakes, Yvonne (Laboratory of Anthropology). *New Mexico Historic Building Inventory—Railroad Survey in Eastern New Mexico County*. Report. Santa Fe: State Historic Preservation Office, 1983.

Office of the Secretary of State. *New Mexico Blue Book 1995–1996*. Santa Fe: Sunstone Press, 1995.

"'Old Chili Line' Recalled by Pioneers of Embudo." *The New Mexican* (September 26, 1965): 5.

Osterwald, Doris B. *Ticket to Toltec: A Mile by Mile Guide for the Cumbres and Toltec Scenic Railraod*. Lakewood, Colo.: Western Guideways, Ltd., 1992.

Perrigo, Lynn. *Oasis on the Pecos: The Town of Eddy and Early Carlsbad*. Available at www.carlsbad.net/mhayes/perrigo.htm.

Poling-Kempes, Lesley. *The Harvey Girls: Women who Opened the West*. New York: Paragon House, 1989.

Potter, Janet Greenstein. *Great American Railroad Stations*. New York: John Wiley and Sons, Inc., 1996.

Pounds, Robert E. *Santa Fe Depots: The Western Lines*. Dallas: Kachina Press, 1984.

Railroad Depot Acquisition and Development. Washington, D.C.: National Trust for Historic Preservation, 1989.

"Railway Men to Stick by Demands: Will Insist upon Eight-Hour Day and a Wage Increase." *Las Vegas Optic*, March 16, 1911.

Ruddle, Richard and Elizabeth Ruddle. "The Railroad Caboose." Available at http://www.warrentoncaboose.org/history/caboose_history.html.

Sandoval, Richard C., William Clark, and Lee Sheck. "Railroads and Railroad Towns in New Mexico." *New Mexico Magazine* (1989).

Seher, Kristine. "Artesia Train Station Leaves Tracks in New Mexico History." *The New Mexican*. October 8, 1987: A11.

Sherman, James E. and Barbara H. Sherman. *Ghost Towns and Mining Camps of New Mexico*. Norman: University of Oklahoma Press, 1975.

Sivinski, Valerie Ann. "Traditions of Depot Building in New Mexico: Wooden Structures." Graduate Thesis, Albuquerque: University of New Mexico, 1979.

Smith, H. Wright. "History of the Stourbridge Lion." *Santa Fe Magazine*, p. 58.

"Social Centers for Railroad Men." *The Chautauquan Magazine* (June 1904).

Southwest Region Timetable: Arizona, New Mexico and West Texas. Pamphlet. Modesto: Altamont Press, n.d.

Spears Architects. *New Mexico Historic Building Inventory—Railroad Survey*. Report. Santa Fe: State Historic Preservation Office, 1993.

Spencer, D. K. "Santa Fe Depots Everywhere, but Not a One to Spare!" Available at www.atsfrr.com/resources/dkspencer/depots.htm.

Standards for Rehabilitation and Guidelines for Rehabilitating Historic Buildings. Washington, D.C.: U.S. Department of the Interior, National Park Service, Preservation Assistance Division, 1990.

Stanley, F. (Stanley Franics Louis Crocchiola). *The Belen, New Mexico Story*. Pantex, Tex.: self-published, 1962.

———. *The Carlsbad, New Mexico Story*. Pep, Tex.: self-published, 1963.

———. *The Clayton, New Mexico Story*. Self-published, 1961.

———. *The Clovis, New Mexico Story*. Pampa, Tex.: self-published, 1966.

———. *The Columbus, New Mexico Story*. Pep, Tex.: self-published, 1966.

———. *The Deming, New Mexico Story*. Pantex, Tex.: self-published, 1962.

———. *The Duke City*. Pampa, Tex.: self-published, 1963.

———. *The Glorieta, New Mexico Story*. Pep, Tex.: self-published, 1965.

———. *The Lake Valley, New Mexico Story*. Pep, Tex.: self-published, 1964.

———. *The Lamy, New Mexico Story*. Pep, Tex.: self-published, 1966.

———. *The Magdalena, New Mexico Story*. Nazareth, Tex.: self-published, 1973.

———. *The Melrose, New Mexico Story*. Pep, Tex.: self-published, 1965.

———. *The Montezuma, New Mexico Story*. Pep, Tex.: self-published, 1963.

———. *The San Antonio, New Mexico Story*. Nazareth, Tex.: self-published, 1973.

———. *Socorro the Oasis*. Denver: World Press, 1950.

Tammariello, Rafael. "Lake Valley: A Silver Town Endures." *Las Cruces Sun News*, Section D, Sunday, November 6, 1977.

To Santa Fe by Narrow Gauge: The Denver & Rio Grande's "Chile Line." Colorado Rail Annual, 1969.

Torry, John. "A Strict Observer." Letter to William H. Brown, Esquire. March 28, 1870.

TRC Mariah Associates, Inc. *Abandoned Railroad Rights of Way Analysis for New Mexico*. Santa Fe: New Mexico State Highway and Transportation Department, February 1996.

Walker, Mike. *Railroad Atlas of North America: Arizona and New Mexico*. Dunkirk, Kent, England: Steam Powered Publishing, 1995.

Wheeler, Keith. *The Railroaders*. New York: Time-Life Books, 1973.

White, Marjorie. "Lake Valley Fame Rests on 'Bridal Chamber.'" The Times Sunday Magazine.

Williams, Philip. *The Clovis Depot: Then and Now*. Pamphlet, n.d.

Wilson, Chris. *The Historic Railroad Buildings of Albuquerque: An Assessment of Significance*. Report prepared for the Redevelopment Division, Planning Department, City of Albuquerque, 1986.

Wilson, Spencer and Vernon Glover. *The Cumbres and Toltec Scenic Railroad: The Historic Preservation Study*. Albuquerque: University of New Mexico Press, 1980.

Wuersching, Marie. *Railroad to Cloudcroft*. Cloudcroft: Sacramento Mountains Historical Society, Inc., 1988.

Index

Note: Page numbers in bold indicate figures.